# JESUS TODAY

## A Spirituality of Radical Freedom

## ALBERT NOLAN

ORBIS E
Maryknoll, New Yo

Founded in 1970, Orbis Books endeavors to publish works that enlighten the mind, nourish the spirit, and challenge the conscience. The publishing arm of the Maryknoll Fathers and Brothers, Orbis seeks to explore the global dimensions of the Christian faith and mission, to invite dialogue with diverse cultures and religious traditions, and to serve the cause of reconciliation and peace. The books published reflect the views of their authors and do not represent the official position of the Maryknoll Society. To learn more about Maryknoll and Orbis Books, please visit our website at www.maryknoll.org.

Copyright © 2006 by Albert Nolan.

Published by Orbis Books, Maryknoll, NY 10545-0308.

Manufactured in the United States of America.

Library of Congress Cataloging-in-Publication Data

Nolan, Albert, 1934–
 Jesus today : a spirituality of radical freedom / Albert Nolan.
   p. cm.
 Includes bibliographical references (p.      ) and index.
 ISBN-13: 978-1-57075-672-6 (pbk.)
 1. Spirituality. 2. Jesus Christ—Person and offices. I. Title.
 BV4501.3.N65 2006
 248.4—dc22
                    2006009475

*Dedicated
to the memory of
Thomas Merton (1915–1968)*

# Contents

# Foreword

## by Timothy Radcliffe, OP

This is a wonderfully fresh and vibrant book. Although Albert Nolan wrote *Jesus Before Christianity* more than thirty years ago, his voice is still strong and youthful. In a world that is hungry for spirituality, we are offered a spirituality that is grounded in the life of Jesus, his own spirituality. It is above all a spirituality of radical freedom.

Albert starts with an analysis of our contemporary culture and the challenges that we face at the beginning of this third millennium. He looks at the profound individualism that subverts our lives and happiness, as well as the effects of globalization, for better or for worse. I found his analysis of the new science especially illuminating. He shows how it invites us to a radically new way of thinking, leaving behind the mechanistic model of the age of Newton. This new science is not a rival to religion, but invites us to see again with wonder and delight.

If we are to face the extraordinary potentialities and perils of this moment, then we need a spirituality that is dynamic and deep. To find this, Albert Nolan takes us back to Jesus. Although I have spent forty years studying and teaching the gospels, I was struck again by Jesus' unending capacity to surprise us and to be always new. We are given a sense of how astonishing was the irruption of this "upside down Messiah" into the world of first-century Judaism.

At the heart of Nolan's understanding of Jesus is his profound relationship with the one whom he called his *abba*. As he explained to me while we drove to Durban earlier this year, this title means nothing so trivial as "Daddy." It is a relationship of the deepest intimacy, beyond gender, without a hint of patriarchalism. "If we find it difficult to take Jesus seriously and to live as he lived, then it is because we have not yet experienced God as our *abba*. The experience of God as his *abba* was the source of Jesus' wisdom, his clarity, his confidence, and his radical freedom. *Without this it is impossible to understand why and how he did the things he did.*"

This is the foundation of the deep mysticism that is at the heart of the life of Jesus. We tend to think that mystics are people who are detached from the real world, with its struggle for justice and even survival. But this book shows that this is not so. Without that radical rooting in the experience of God, we have nothing to say to our contemporaries and we shall be impotent before the challenges of our time. Again and again I have found that the contemporary theologians who are most perceptive of the political, economic, and ecological crisis of this moment are also those who are most deeply rooted in the mystical tradition. Among my brethren in the Dominican Order one thinks not only of Albert Nolan but also of Edward Schillebeeckx and Gustavo Gutiérrez.

Albert also explores the silence and solitude that were part of the life of Jesus, his mediation of God's forgiveness and, most beautifully, the role of women in his life. Resisting the loony imaginings of the *Da Vinci Code*, Albert shows us how deep was Jesus' relationship with Mary Magdalene, the first patron of the Dominican Order, and with Mary his mother.

On the basis of this double analysis, of the challenges of our society and the spirituality of Jesus, Albert then proposes a practical spirituality for today, one that offers a way forward for anyone, regardless of how busy or immersed in the daily affairs of our world he or she may be. In fact one of the first challenges that we are offered is that of resisting the temptation of busyness, what Herbert McCabe called "the tyranny of work." We need to be liberated from the imperialism of the ego, which would make us the center of the world, and which destroys our sense of flourishing only with and for other people, and indeed the whole of creation.

We are invited to form within ourselves a "grateful heart." Meister Eckhart, a fourteenth-century Dominican, once said, "If the only prayer I ever say is Thank You...that is enough." Albert writes beautifully about the childlike quality of Jesus, which frees us to be playful and which is the very opposite of childishness. He explores the difference between playfulness and hypocrisy. "There is a superficial similarity between playfulness and hypocrisy. Both involve pretending to be what one is not. The difference is that the hypocrite is serious, while the child does it for fun. The hypocrite is living a lie. The child knows the truth, and that is what makes it funny. In fact, the best way to deal with one's hypocritical ego is to learn to laugh at it."

We must learn the art of detachment. This is not a cold rejection of affection and intimacy, but the art of learning not to cling. I was myself challenged by Albert's insistence on the need to become detached from *time*. Whenever anyone comes to see us, that is the right time. We must even learn to be detached from God. Albert writes superbly: "Trusting God, as Jesus did, does not mean clinging to God; it means letting go of everything so as to surrender ourselves and our lives to God. There is a difference between attachment and surrender. In the end we must become detached from God too. We must let go of God in order to jump into the embrace of a loving Father whom we can trust implicitly. We don't need *to hold on* tightly, because we will *be held*—like a child in the arms of its parents." Above all, there is the training in forgiveness. This is not a forgiveness that closes its eyes to the scandals and injustices of this world. It is clear-eyed and truthful. But it summons us beyond the imputation of blame and guilt.

The penultimate chapter on becoming "one with the Universe" is especially stimulating. Even someone with as little scientific formation as myself can get a glimpse of the vast possibilities of our emerging understanding of our world. Albert rightly points out that young people today are rarely interested in dogma and doctrine. This is so. And yet one can glimpse here the intimations of a new doctrine of creation that is not stuffy, that does not cramp our thought but liberates our imagination, and, as all good doctrine should, invites us to continue along the path toward the mystery.

Finally, we are brought back to the underlying theme of the entire book, which is freedom. We are invited to taste the freedom that was Jesus', the freedom that was founded on his utter trust in his *abba*. The most widely shared value of modernity is that of freedom. It is often understood in terms of personal autonomy, a freedom that locks us in solitude and that justifies the narcissistic egoism of our times. Here we glimpse the freedom for which Christ has set us free, to quote St. Paul. The growth in this freedom is a slow process. Albert reminds us that "the human child takes longer than the offspring of other animals to grow up and mature. This is because there is much more to learn. Most of what we need to know to be mature adults comes from culture rather than instinct. We need a long period of education and training before we can stand on our own feet and make decisions for ourselves. During our childhood we need rules and laws." This book offers us a pedagogy in freedom, the fruit of which is a touch of the spontaneity and the lightheartedness of Jesus.

When I first met Albert, more than twenty years ago, I was a young prior of Blackfriars, Oxford. I confess that I was a little nervous about the visit by this famous theologian. Surely he would find us all rather lax in our commitment to the poor, rather inadequate, and mediocre! But it was not thus. We discovered a brother who was truthful, utterly himself, and yet with whom we could feel at ease, visiting pubs, laughing, and enjoying his company. This is the Albert whom one can still encounter in this book, fresh, hopeful and strong, and immensely understanding of us all as we limp, or sometimes run, toward the Kingdom.

# Preface

Some thirty years ago I wrote a book called *Jesus Before Christianity*. My aim had been to help the reader appreciate something of what Jesus might have meant to his contemporaries in the early years of the first century, before he became enshrined in doctrine, dogma, and ritual.

Much has happened since then in the world, in South Africa, and in my own life. In 1988 I wrote *God in South Africa: The Challenge of the Gospel*. It was an exercise in contextual theology and the context was apartheid South Africa. But four years later we witnessed the dismantling of the whole system of apartheid.

In the meantime, the feminist perspective opened my eyes to many things, including aspects of Jesus' life that I had not noticed before. Recent archaeological discoveries have given us a clearer picture of the context in which Jesus lived. The new science and in particular the new cosmology have given us a stunning, new vision of God's grandeur and creativity. And yet at the same time the destruction of the environment and the threat of extinction have worsened.

Along the way I also became more aware of the need we all have for personal liberation and therefore spirituality. The need for social liberation remains as urgent as ever and, although much progress has been made in this direction—especially in South Africa—what we now see is how the gains we have made can be undermined by a lack of personal inner freedom. More often than not our self-centered egos seem to get in the way. We need a new spirituality and more and more people are discovering that.

What I now offer the reader is a book entitled *Jesus Today: A Spirituality of Radical Freedom*. My aim this time is to look more specifically at what Jesus might mean to you and me and our contemporaries in the twenty-first century. It is a book about spirituality, Jesus' own spirituality, which I have chosen to call a spirituality of radical freedom. And because it is about spirituality, I will focus on matters that were not touched upon in my earlier works—such as Jesus' contemplative prayer and his concern for the individual. This book is also contextual, but the context this time is today's world and not just South Africa.

I am indebted to countless numbers of people who have helped me and inspired me in a variety of ways over the years. Most immediately, I am grateful to those who read the draft or parts of it and gave me invaluable advice: Larry Kaufman, Marguerite Bester, Mark James, Leslie Dikeni, and Judy Connors. In the background while I was writing the book in 2005 I had the indispensable support of my Dominican community in Pietermaritzburg. They provided me with the time and the space to read and write—undisturbed! I thank them for that.

There is no way that I could ever express my indebtedness to my Dominican brothers and sisters, religious and lay, locally and internationally, for the formation, teaching, encouragement, and inspiration that they have given me over the last fifty-five years. Without that I would never have contemplated putting pen to paper as I have dared to do again and again. It is in this context that I am particularly grateful to my Dominican brother, Timothy Radcliffe, for writing the foreword to this book.

But it was not only my Dominican family that formed and inspired me over the years. There were two other powerfully formative influences: the Young Christian Students movement and the heroes of the South African struggle against apartheid. From the student movement I learnt the pedagogical method known as See-Judge-Act. For that I remain forever grateful.

More powerful still was the example of the political giants of our struggle. I am thinking of men and women like Nelson

Mandela, Albert Luthuli, Oliver Tambo, Walter Sisulu, Steve Biko, Chris Hani, Albertina Sisulu, Helen Joseph, Joe Slovo, and church leaders like Desmond Tutu, Beyers Naude, and Denis Hurley. What inspired me was not only their courage and commitment in the struggle for social and political freedom, but also, and more important, *their humility and personal freedom*. Without their example I might never have set out on the path of study and reflection that led to the writing of this book.

Finally, there are the many authors whose writings have contributed to the thinking in this book: Jesus scholars, mystics, spiritual writers, psychologists, cosmologists, and political analysts. I am indebted to them too. And in a very special way I am indebted to Pierre Bester for introducing me to recent psychological/spiritual authors like A. H. Almaas, Sandra Maitri, and Ken Wilber.

Albert Nolan
Pietermaritzburg RSA
2006

# Introduction

On the whole we don't take Jesus seriously—whether we call ourselves Christians or not. There are some remarkable exceptions, but by and large we don't love our enemies, we don't turn the other cheek, we don't forgive seventy times seven times, we don't bless those who curse us, we don't share what we have with the poor, and we don't put all our hope and trust in God. We have our excuses. I am no saint. It is not meant for everybody, surely? It's a great ideal, but it's not very practical in this day and age.

My proposal will be that we learn to take Jesus seriously, and that it is precisely in this day and age that we need to do so. In fact, what we also need to take seriously *is* this day and age, our times. We too often live in a kind of dream world that does not take the threats and challenges of today seriously enough. There are Christians who think that one can take Jesus seriously without taking too much notice of what is happening in the world around us. Jesus' spirituality was thoroughly contextual. He read the signs of his times and taught his followers to do the same (Mt 16:3-4 par). We take Jesus seriously when, among other things, we begin to read the signs of our times with honesty and sincerity.

Reading the signs of our times is not a matter of looking at our world from the outside as if we were not part of it. We are inextricably enmeshed in its web of relationships. It is our world and we cannot have any kind of serious spirituality except in our world.

In Part One, therefore, I outline my own reading of the signs of our times. In Part Two I take a closer look at Jesus' own spirituality, while in Parts Three and Four I begin to look at the practicalities of living in the context of today a spirituality inspired by Jesus.

The focus of this book, then, is spirituality. Judging from the large number of books on the subject of spirituality that can be found in almost any bookshop these days, there is an unprecedented interest in matters of the spirit. However, much that is written about spirituality tends to marginalize Jesus or even reject him as irrelevant. On the other hand, those who treat Jesus as central to their spirituality tend to make him the object of their spirituality rather than a person who had a spirituality of his own from which we might be able to learn something. We will not be able to appreciate the full significance of Jesus for our present struggles without a deeper appreciation of his spirituality.

I would like to show how the new and exciting avenues that are being opened up to us by the events and discoveries of our time make the living of Jesus' spirit of love and freedom a serious possibility for many more people than those who are already living that spirit. I would even like to suggest that Jesus' spirituality might be more relevant in this day and age than ever before. I will argue that Jesus' spirituality can be called a spirituality of radical freedom and that this is of particular relevance today. My endeavor will be to propose a practical spirituality for our time, a spirituality that is rooted in Jesus' spirituality.

My focus is spirituality, not theology. We may deplore the present divorce between spirituality and theology, but since it is spirituality that deals with experience and practice, and theology that deals with doctrines and dogmas, my concern in this book is decidedly spiritual. This is not a book about Christology, the theological significance of Jesus' life, death, and resurrection. It is a book about Jesus' own spirituality, that is to say, about the experience and attitudes behind what he said and did, what fired and inspired him.

While some attention will have to be given to the historical details of Jesus' life, I do not wish to enter into the modern debates about the historical Jesus. We have more than enough evidence to enable us to read between the lines and extrapolate the outlines of a spirituality. Often it is not important to know whether Jesus said this or that, because in either case his attitude to life and to people was the same. Similarly, the stories that were put together by the gospel writers can be powerful confirmations of Jesus' particular spirituality, even if the stories themselves do not conform to some people's norms for historical accuracy.

What has been particularly helpful though, has been recent research into the cultural, social, political, and economic context in which Jesus developed and lived out his spirituality. Archaeological research as a result of extensive diggings in Galilee and Judea, and more generally around the Mediterranean, has cast much light on the way the Roman Empire was encroaching on the lives of everyone from peasants to kings.[1] Such research has also confirmed the present emphasis in Jesus studies on the fact that he was a Galilean peasant and a Jew.[2] Such information is useful for extrapolating his spirituality from the available evidence.

Another of the debates that I have not entered into in this book concerns the similarities and differences between Jesus' spirituality and that of other faiths, religions, and worldviews. Although I have sometimes mentioned a similarity and taken note of Jesus' closeness to the traditions of the Hebrew Scriptures, for the most part I have focused quite simply on Jesus' spirituality itself, avoiding comparisons as much as possible.

I write in the first place for my fellow Christians in all their present-day diversity and dividedness, but not only for them. I have in mind also those who no longer go to church and those who have decided that they can no longer call themselves Christians. I have tried to write for those who are searching for a relevant spirituality, and for those who are not at all sure that they need a spirituality; for those who cling to religious beliefs and practices, and for those who have given up all such things. Writing for such a wide and varied readership is extremely difficult, if not impossible. But I have tried to do so because I am deeply convinced that Jesus' spirituality is singularly relevant to the unprecedented drama of today's world.

# I
# THE SIGNS OF OUR TIMES

The following four chapters cannot count as much more than a *glimpse* at the extremely complex and ever-shifting signs of our times. Yet even a cursory glance at what is happening today will enable us to see that the signs of our times are, to say the least, *startling*—not only because we can now see that we are living on the edge of chaos, but also because a giant leap forward in our history and our evolution seems to have become a real possibility.

The signs of our times are ambiguous. Things seem to be moving in several different directions at the same time. Some trends seem to be reactions to the direction others are taking. The different signs become like strands of wool that are woven together into a complex pattern. What we see today is the pattern as it is at this particular moment in the long history of the unfolding of the universe.

The signs of the times are pointers to the future. It is not that they show us clearly and definitively where we are going. Rather, the value of these pointers is that they challenge us. And what matters here is that we *allow* them to challenge us. Or, to put it in terms of faith, what matters is that we allow God to challenge us through our reading of the signs. What we have to

1

avoid is the imposition of our pre-conceived ideas upon the reality of today. Our aim must be to face the truth about what is actually happening—whether we like it or not. Pointing fingers and finding people to blame for today's problems will simply blind us to the significance of the signs we are looking at.

The four chapters of Part One will help us to establish what we mean by "today." After that we will explore the relevance of Jesus.

CHAPTER 1

# Hunger for Spirituality

Published early in 2004, Dan Brown's *The Da Vinci Code* has become the biggest selling novel in history.[1] And the movie is set to break any number of box office records. What is it about our times that makes books and movies of this kind so extraodinarily popular?

*The Da Vinci Code* is a historical novel. However, it abounds in historical errors and displays considerable ignorance when it comes to the history of art and the structures of the Catholic Church. It has released an avalanche of criticism from academics, ecclesiastics, theologians, and especially historians.[2] But this just seems to add to its appeal.

In Dan Brown's novel, the great secret, kept hidden for two thousand years but handed down in a code known to only a few people, is that Jesus married Mary Magdalene and they had a child called Sarah, and that this royal bloodline continues down to this day. It makes for an intriguing storyline, especially in view of the present-day scholarly interest in the role of Mary Magdalene in the early church.[3]

The significance of *The Da Vinci Code*, however, is not to be found in the accuracy or inaccuracy of its contents, but in the book's accuracy as a barometer of where we are today and what people are looking for. More and more people, and especially young people, have given up all the certainties of the past: religious certainties, scientific certainties, cultural certainties, political certainties, and historical certainties. Everything is being questioned. They feel that one can no longer believe anything that authorities of any kind are saying and have been saying for centuries. Ours is an age of unprecedented skepticism. One opinion is as good as another. All one can say is that some opinions are old and boring, while others are *interesting*.

Readers are fascinated by *The Da Vinci Code* because it rides roughshod over certainties or supposed certainties of the past and offers a story that is much more intriguing. Revelations about what might really have happened in the past are interesting. They may or may not be true, but they are at least not slavishly following some infallible authority, religious or secular. *The Da Vinci Code* is experienced as freeing the imagination to consider any number of other possibilities. It liberates the mind from what is perceived as the straitjacket of imposed certainties and dogmas.

Academics call this attitude of mind *postmodernism*, and the popularity of *The Da Vinci Code* is a barometer or measure of just how widespread this way of thinking is. It is a sign of our times.

## Postmodernism

Modernity was the age of reason that began with what is generally known as the Enlightenment. It coincided more or less with the scientific age shaped by Newton's mechanistic worldview.[4] It has also been the age of industrial capitalism and unlimited economic growth. Modernity's optimism about the future was based upon the absolute certainty that the progress of science, technology, and reason would overcome all human problems, and that pre-modern religious superstition and the belief in magic would gradually fade away. Religion, morality, and art were relegated to the sphere of private belief. What really mattered for the human race was economic and political progress.

Gradually, during the first half of the twentieth century, modernity's house of cards began to collapse. Even the most industrially advanced countries, such as Germany under the Nazis and other Fascist states around the world, began to act irrationally and inhumanly. Their violence, cruelty, and methods of torture could simply not be squared with the ideals of human progress.

At the same time, the Communist bloc of nations, with its own form of modernity and its own vision of human progress, began to manifest the same kind of totalitarianism and oppression. Toward the end of the century these regimes collapsed, leaving us with one superpower that now seems to be hell-bent on war to wipe out terrorism while it ignores the ecological destruction of the earth. Is this human progress?

No wonder we now have a generation that is skeptical about any ideology at all. No grand narratives, they say. No schemes for saving the world. They don't work.

Religious ideologies have suffered the same fate. Scandals have rocked the churches and undermined their authority. For many people today, all religious authorities seem to be exclusive, divisive, and oppressive (especially of women). On the other hand, the scientific rationalism of the past that excluded all miracles is also being questioned. There is a fascination with vampires, aliens, and magic, with the occult, the supernatural, and the preternatural. People don't necessarily believe in any of these things, they are just fascinated by them. Hence the phenomenal interest in Harry Potter, the child magician, and other similar books.

Deep down, though, most people today feel totally *insecure*. All we ever seem to hear is bad news: wars, murder, abuse, institutional violence, terrorism and our destruction of the environment, not to mention earthquakes, tsunamis, and hurricanes. In the face of all this, feelings of insecurity and hopelessness are inevitable. Most human beings today live in a state of suppressed despair, trying to find ways of distracting themselves from the hard realities of our times. As the spiritual writer Joanna Macy puts it, "A dread of what is happening to our future stays on the fringes of awareness, too deep to name and too fearsome to face."[5]

In the past, most people relied on the certainties and practices of their respective cultures. Today, all traditional cultures are slowly disintegrating: Western cultures, African cultures, Asian cultures, and smaller indigenous cultures. There is nothing much left for people to hang onto. We are slowly sinking. Blaming this one or that one is of no help in a situation like this.

Some turn to drink or drugs. Some commit suicide. Some still find their imagined security in wealth and possessions. Others, quite understandably, use sport, entertainment, or sex to divert attention from the worries of life.

One very strong response to the uncertainties of life in our postmodern world is the attempt to return to the past.

## The Return to the Past

Fundamentalism is a particularly vigorous, appealing, and dangerous attempt to return to the fundamentals of the past, or to what seem to have been the fundamentals of the past. In the past there was certainty, authority, and absolute truth. This manifested itself most of all in religious dogma. It is not surprising then, in our present state of uncertainty and insecurity, to find people resorting to religious fundamentalism: Christian fundamentalism, Muslim fundamentalism, Hindu fundamentalism, and Jewish fundamentalism. Each of these is different and often in open conflict with at least some of the others. What all have in common is a reliance upon an authority that provides absolute truths—truths that cannot be questioned or doubted. This is the kind of security they offer to a very insecure world.

Fundamentalism often takes on a political form. More accurately, militant governments and militant resistance groups often make use of religious fundamentalism: some American politicians make use of Christian fundamentalism; militant resistance in the Middle East sometimes makes use of Muslim fundamentalism; at one stage, the governing party in India made use of Hindu fundamentalism; and Israel utilizes a kind of Jewish fundamentalism. This use of fundamentalism often leads to violence: institutional state violence or revolutionary and even terrorist violence.

Neo-conservatism is another response to the frightening insecurities of our times. It is also a return to the past, a return to the principles, practices, customs, beliefs, and sense of identity that made some of us feel so safe and secure in the past. A good example of this is the neo-conservative backlash in the Catholic Church following on the liberating reforms of the Second Vatican Council after 1965.

Despite the failures of modernity, a very large number of people are still stuck in it and still believe in its promises of progress. Leaders in the so-called developing nations are busy "industrializing" and "modernizing" their countries—in other words, becoming Western.

There is yet another response to postmodernism, a response that is gaining momentum every day. It is the search for an appropriate spirituality.

## Spirituality

In our present circumstances of uncertainty and insecurity, spirituality could be seen as yet another form of escape. While this may be true in some cases, it seems to me that by and large the new search for spirituality, the deep hunger for spirituality, is genuine and sincere. It is one of the signs of our times.

The sign, however, is not the number of people who have found a satisfactory form of spirituality to live by. Some have done so, but the sign is rather the widespread *hunger* for spirituality, the search for spirituality, the felt need for spirituality. One could argue that all human beings need, and have always needed, spirituality. What is happening today is that many more people are becoming acutely *aware* of their need for spirituality.

This need or hunger is experienced in a variety of ways. Some experience it as the need for something that will give them the inner strength to cope with life, or peace of mind and freedom from feelings of fear and anxiety. Others experience it in seeing themselves falling apart and in need of something bigger than themselves to hold them together. There is also a sense of being wounded, hurt, broken, and in need of healing. Many, it seems, feel cut off and isolated from other people and from nature. They long for connection and harmony. An increasing number of people, especially young people, feel the need to be in contact with the *mystery* beyond what we can see, hear, smell, taste, touch, or think, beyond the constraints of mechanistic materialism.[6] Some experience the hunger for spirituality quite simply as a longing for God.

To explore further the complexities of this hunger, we can look at some of the spiritualities that have risen or have been revived in recent times. This has sometimes happened within a particular religious tradition, and sometimes outside of any specific religious institution.

## From within Religious Traditions

During the second half of the twentieth century, in the midst of our growing uncertainty and insecurity, the person who was responsible, more than anyone else, for reviving and popularizing the Catholic tradition of contemplative spirituality was the American writer and monk, Thomas Merton. He enabled millions of Catholics, and others, to grow up spiritually as he himself had done—step by step.

As a young man, Merton embodied the spirit of his time with its confusion and anxieties. What followed was his famous conversion, his rejection of the world and his escape into a strict, old-fashioned monastery. But then as his spiritual journey matured he turned again to embrace in a new way the world he had rejected. From his monastic enclosure he got involved in the American civil rights movement and anti-war campaigns, and he grew in appreciation of the mysticism of Eastern religions.

Thomas Merton died in 1968, but his many writings have continued to feed the spiritual hunger of new generations of seekers worldwide.

During the same period, the second half of the twentieth century, the spiritual hunger of the West was also being fed by Eastern religions, especially in the form of yoga and meditation. Meditation of one kind or another has become very popular, although it is only recently that the ancient Christian tradition of meditation has been rediscovered and popularized. It is known to a growing number of people today as "centering prayer."

But the really powerful development of spirituality within Christianity, and more generally in the Western world and elsewhere, has been the discovery of the relevance and importance of *mysticism*.


## Mysticism

There was a time when the mystics were regarded as rather odd people whose writings were singularly irrelevant to the concerns and needs of our world. Today that view has been reversed. An increasing number of people are now reading the mystics, both Western and Eastern, studying them in their historical contexts, publishing critical editions of their writings,

and finding in them a deep resonance with our postmodern insecurities and uncertainties.[7] The works of medieval mystics
such as Meister Eckhart, Hildegard of Bingen, Julian of Norwich,
Catherine of Siena, the anonymous author of *The Cloud of
Unknowing,* and the famous Spanish mystics like Teresa of
Avila, John of the Cross, and Ignatius of Loyola, to name but a
few, are to be found on the shelves of our bookshops alongside
the works of our modern mystics such as Thomas Merton and
Thich Nhat Hanh.

Mystics are not extraordinary people who perform superhu-
man feats and get carried away by weird, miraculous experiences. Mystics are appreciated today as people who take God
seriously. They do not merely believe in the existence of God or
the divine, they claim to have *experienced* the presence of God
in their lives and in the world. The aim and purpose of mysticism is union with God, a oneness with the divine that is complete and total. For mystics, everything else follows from this.
When the mysterious presence of God fills their consciousness
in ways that are impossible to describe, their lives are transformed. They become happy, joyful, confident, humble, loving,
free, and secure. The hunger for spirituality is a hunger for precisely that.

One of the features of the mystical experience of union with
God is that it always includes an experience of oneness with all
human beings and with the whole universe. Francis of Assisi,
for example, felt completely at one with all his human brothers
and sisters, as well as with Brother Sun and Sister Moon. People
today are fascinated and deeply moved by the mystical experience of oneness. But what attracts attention more than anything
else is the claim that mystical union is a religious *experience*
rather than a religious *dogma.*

The move from ideas and thoughts to experience, from in-
tellectual knowledge to felt knowledge has long been part of
human history.[8] In postmodernism it has reached an unprecedented high point. The demand is for experience, not grand

ideas. And the mystics have always been *the* great proponents
of deep religious experience.

In its origins, Pentecostalism was also an expression of the
hunger for an experience of God. Here and in the broad charis-
matic movement that has swept through Christianity since the
second half of the twentieth century, spirituality is experienced
as the outpouring of the Holy Spirit. What matters is the concrete experience of the gifts of the Spirit—from joy to speaking
in tongues. Whatever one may think of this, it must be seen as
part of the overall hunger for spiritual experience.


**The Hunger for Healing**

Another very significant way in which the hunger for spirituality finds expression in the world today is in the desperate
need felt by so many people for *healing*. This is particularly
true in Africa. In 2004, an estimated two million people gathered on the beaches near Lagos in Nigeria hoping to receive
healing of one kind or another from a well-known Nigerian
healer. In Nairobi I once witnessed a gathering of about a million people covering the campus and the sports fields of the
university, watching, on closed circuit television screens, a visiting American faith healer. In Africa, churches that offer healing
are growing exponentially. This is not because of their success
rate as far as actual healing is concerned. It is because they speak
to the desperate hunger for healing.

Nor is this phenomenon confined to Africa. Faith-healers
can be found everywhere. The Catholic Church tends to have
shrines for healing rather than faith healers in such places as
Lourdes, Fatima, Medjugorje. In India and Sri Lanka there are
holy places and holy rivers where people can go for healing.

Most of the time what we are looking at here is the need for
healing from "physical" ailments or injuries. There is nothing
new about that. What is significant is that today, while more and

more people are making use of Western medicine, they feel the need for something more, something transcendent, something that will heal body, soul, and society—holistic healing.

For some time now Westerners have been going to their therapists for psychological healing. The practice has been that if you have a physical illness you go to your medical doctor, but when you experience the need for inner peace, inner strength, and wholeness you go to your therapist. Now, Westerners are beginning to feel the need for something more than psychotherapy.

### Secular Spirituality

One of the most significant developments of our time is the separation of spirituality from religion. Diarmuid O'Murchu, among others, argues that while spirituality has been with us from the beginning, religion was introduced only five thousand years ago, and it will gradually disappear because spirituality is now flourishing outside of the great world religions.[9]

While something very significant is happening here, I do not think that setting up a dichotomy between the words "spirituality" and "religion" is particularly valuable in our search for the signs of our times. Reseachers like Mircea Eliade refer to what has been happening from the beginning as religion, and postmodern philosophers like Jacques Derrida write about what is happening today outside of any church or institution as religion or as religious experience. What we are all beginning to recognize is that religious institutions tend to become fossilized, legalistic, dogmatic, and authoritarian.[10] But, whatever we choose to call it, there is a very powerful hunger for spirituality today that cannot find the nourishment it seeks in our churches, mosques, synagogues, or temples.

One of the places where the hunger for spirituality is felt most acutely is among those who have discovered the new universe story, which we will look at in chapter 4. The grandeur and glory of God or of the sacred is powerfully manifested in the unfolding mystery of the universe. The search here is for a practical spirituality that will enable us to live this out in daily life and, for those who are Christians, in the church.

Many church-going Christians write off the secular search for spirituality as New Age. In fact, there is no one coherent spirituality or movement that can be labeled "New Age." What we have is a growing number of spiritual searchers who are willing to try anything, whether it is called paganism, or magic, or superstition, or animism, or pantheism, or whatever else. The variety is enormous. Some of the rites and practices are indeed childish.[11] At the same time, those who do resort to "spiritual technologies" are often exploited by entrepreneurs who find ways of making money out of the insatiable religious curiosity of some seekers.[12]

On the other hand, there are some powerfully simple spiritual insights, like those contained in William Bloom's holistic approach to understanding the new spirituality emerging in our world,[13] that can also be classified as New Age. Should we not see the whole phenomenon as yet another manifestation of the hunger for spirituality?

David Tacey's research into the spirituality of Australian youth today can help us to understand what is happening among young people throughout the world. Today's secularized youth are reaching out beyond a scientific and mechanistic worldview in search of the great mystery that underpins it all.[14] This is something they do not experience in their traditional churches, they say. All they find there are authoritarian teachings, empty rituals, and dualism. The body-soul dualism is meaningless to postmodern youth. They want a spirituality that includes the body and its sexuality.[15]

My own experience of youth, black and white, at school and university, over more than thirty years, is that none of them, except the fundamentalists and religious neo-conservatives, are

any longer interested in doctrines and dogmas. The phenomenal success of Taizé, the ecumenical monastery and retreat center
in France where, throughout the year, thousands of young people
gather for a week at a time, is due to the freedom it provides. No
doctrines or dogmas are imposed. There are no sermons at all in
any of the long liturgies. The young people gather in groups to
discuss spirituality or the Bible or whatever they want. There
are long periods of silence, and the prayers, the songs, and the
worship services are simple and quietly repetitive.

Whatever we may feel about all this, it must be recognized
as one of the signs of our times.

## CHAPTER 2

# The Crisis of Individualism

The cultural ideal of the Western industrialized world is the self-made, self-sufficient, autonomous individual who stands by himself or herself, not needing anyone else (except for sex) and not beholden to anyone for anything. He or she may consult a doctor or a therapist or a lawyer, but because these services are purchased, one can still see oneself as autonomous. Having one's own money is of course crucial to maintaining this kind of independence. Hence the careerism and feverish busyness that characterize the autonomous lifestyle.

This is the ideal that people live and work for. It is their goal in life, and they will sacrifice anything to achieve it. This is how you "get a life for yourself." This is how you discover your identity. As one author has described it: "The Western world maintains that an individual attains authentic identity only if clearly separated from others and from the rest of the enveloping world."[1] Freedom and happiness are equated with independence and self-sufficiency.

From the point of view of all other cultures in the world, past and present, this is simply unintelligible. In other cultures, the person who is separated and isolated from the rest of the community would be regarded as very unfortunate. Interdependence, social coherence, and reliance upon one another are highly appreciated cultural values. In Africa we say: "A person becomes a person through other people." In other words, your identity depends upon the family, the friends, and the community who relate to you and to whom you relate.

There have been plenty of people in the past with inflated egos—kings, conquerors, and other dictators—but in the Western world today the cultivation of the ego is seen as the ideal for everyone. Individualism permeates almost everything we do. It is a basic assumption. It is like a cult. We worship the ego.

Western individualism is spreading throughout the world. It is part of neo-liberal globalization and it is destroying other more communitarian cultures in its wake. In Africa we are witnessing the inevitable growth of individualism, especially in economic matters. This is not said by way of blame or condemnation. Western culture has developed in this way and we will need to ask how it happened. It doesn't help to blame anyone for it.

Individualism itself is not new. What is new, and is one of the important signs of our times, is the growing awareness that narcissistic individualism is psychologically, socially, politically, economically, spiritually, and ecologically *destructive*.

## The Destructiveness of Individualism

From 1979 to 1984 a team of sociologists led by Robert Bellah did extensive research into the psychosocial effects of individualism in the United States. Their findings were shocking. The effects included alienation, loneliness, lovelessness, unhappiness, and an inability to maintain relationships.[2]

In this individualistic culture, therapists and counselors have seen their task as that of helping the individual to develop his or her ego in order to reach the great Western ideal of *self-fulfillment*. Today psychologists are beginning to realize that this leads only to self-centeredness and narcissism, which are themselves the cause of mental illnesses both neurotic and psychotic.[3] The self-centered individualist loses touch with reality.

It is now recognized that the "me-generation" is thoroughly unhealthy. This is the generation of Westerners who were born during the baby boom after the Second World War and grew up in the flower power protests of the 1960s. Their aim in life was, and often still is, self-fulfillment. Today authors like Ken Wilber see such self-fulfillment as a debilitating form of self-centeredness. He calls it "boomeritis."[4]

Many of today's young people feel that, despite all this individualism, their egos have been suppressed. They continue to claim the freedom to do their own thing, to be themselves, to express themselves, to assert themselves, to "get attitude."

Too often the search for spirituality, especially among youth in the Western world, is undertaken in a manner that is also self-centered. A thoroughly individualist spirituality is proving to be counter-productive. More and more people who have been reflecting on their own experience of spirituality are discovering what the mystics have always said, that we must undertake the painful and difficult task of moving beyond our self-centeredness, our individualism, and our egos. Programs that ignore this truth and offer a self-fulfillment or follow-your-bliss kind of spirituality are totally misleading. Moreover, too many of the people who set themselves up as gurus have swollen egos themselves. Such programs and gurus are not able to satisfy a genuine hunger for spirituality.

In Europe, North America, and Australia, churches are empty. On the other hand, in the rest of the world and especially in Africa the churches are packed to overflowing and both Christianity and Islam are growing fast. This is not simply a return to the past, to fundamentalism. My guess is that it is a search for spirituality and healing in the solidarity of a community.

In Africa and in the African diaspora people huddle together in church services to support one another and to feel the oneness of harmonized singing and praying. In Western-type

churches everybody sits as far as possible from everybody else.
There is no huddling together.

It is the difference between *ubuntu* (becoming a person in
and through other people) and Western individualism (becoming
a person by being as independent as possible of other people).
Some of us believe that we find God together, while others believe we must search alone. The former might want to be together in a church or some other worshiping community. The
latter try to develop their spirituality in private. In this regard,
David Tacey warns us about what he calls "the appalling loneliness that a privatized spirituality can bring."[5]

There is a similar problem in many of the struggles for justice. What more and more people are discovering is that without personal liberation or inner freedom, our hard-won social
freedoms are undermined and perverted by selfish individualism. If the people who have been socially liberated are not also
liberated from their own egos, their personal selfishness, they
are in danger of repeating—in another form—the very oppression and cruelty against which they have fought.

While the concept of human rights has contributed enormously to a more just world, it too is a somewhat individualistic concept. Human rights are the rights of the individual. There
is a growing recognition that we need to be working for something more like the common good.[6] Our culture of individualism even in struggles for justice often sees the common good
as working against the interests of the individual. That is not
true. The common good is always in the best interests of the individual too.

Worse still is the abuse of the right to private ownership.
The right to private ownership makes it illegal for a poor person to steal a loaf of bread but perfectly legal for a rich man to
hoard more food and other resources than he or she can ever
make use of. Rampant individualism leads to the limitless ac-
cumulation of wealth by some while billions of others live in
misery and die of starvation. The rich justify this blatant injus-

tice by claiming their right to own as much as they like, no matter how many others are deprived of the bare necessities of life. "I earned it all without breaking any laws," they say. "It is *mine,* and I am not responsible for the lives of other people." This must be one of the most destructive consequences of individualism. It destroys millions of people every day.

The tragic irony of Western individualism is that it now threatens the very freedom it hoped to achieve.[7] Individualism and separation have led us, in the words of Robert Bellah, "to the brink of disaster."[8] Nowhere is the destructiveness of selfish individualism manifested more clearly, dangerously, and dramatically than in our destruction of the environment. Ecologically, Western individualism has brought us to the edge of chaos.

## The Destruction of the Earth

In 1995, Richard Leakey and Roger Lewin wrote a book entitled *The Sixth Extinction: Biodiversity and Its Survival.* They had made a study of the mass extinctions that had taken place on planet earth over millions of years including the most famous of them, the fifth extinction, when the dinosaurs were wiped out. That was some sixty-five million years ago. The sixth extinction is the one we are heading for now, only this time it is unlikely to be caused by an asteroid smashing into the earth. This time it will be the result of human selfishness.

We all know the story of environmental destruction: the pollution of rivers and oceans, the destruction of forests, the erosion of topsoil, the rapid desertification of parts of the earth, the greenhouse effect created by the burning of fossil fuels, the destruction of species, the over-fishing along our coasts, the effects of the population explosion in so-called developing nations, the dangers of nuclear waste and the unknown and perhaps irreversible effects of genetic engineering. A veritable litany of woes.

We have been talking about these threats for decades. Beginning in 1962 with Rachel Carson's book, *The Silent Spring,* we have been discovering new ways in which our earth and our species are dying. There has been some response to the warnings, but nowhere near enough to stem the tide.[9]

The most recent scientific discovery, however, is not about some future catastrophe. It is about the disaster that is already happening—*global warming.* I want to focus on this because I believe that it is one of the outstanding signs of our times.

## Global Warming

Scientists tell us that the burning of fossil fuels (oil, coal, and gas) emits carbon dioxide into the atmosphere. We have been doing this since the Industrial Revolution and at an ever-increasing rate. At present, such emissions send seven billion tons of carbon dioxide into the atmosphere every year.

All of this is collecting around the globe like a giant blanket that has the effect of warming the earth beyond the normal temperatures of the past. It is known as the greenhouse effect. There has always been a thin, delicately balanced blanket of carbon dioxide up there, but since the Industrial Revolution we have increased the thickness of this blanket by 30 percent.

To some, global warming may sound innocent enough. But scientists, and especially meteorologists, tell us that it will cause—and is already causing—extreme weather conditions: devastating droughts in some places, killer floods in other places, widespread failure of agriculture and therefore food scarcity, and, most destructive of all for the human race, the rising of sea levels everywhere.

Sea levels will rise, first of all, because the warming of the oceans will expand the volume of water. More dramatically, however, the melting of icebergs and icecaps in the Arctic and Antarctic will produce sea levels that are many feet higher than at present. That will mean the end of all our coastal cities from New York and London to Lagos, all the low-lying islands on the planet, and practically the whole of countries like Bangladesh.

At first it was thought that such results were still a long way off. But at a conference of scientists (not environmental activists) called together by the British Government (not the Green Party) in 2005, it was announced that global warming is happening much faster than had been anticipated and that the West Antarctic ice sheet might start breaking up far sooner than previously thought. That alone would cause the oceans to rise by sixteen feet (4.88 meters) everywhere[10]—a permanent, world-wide, giant tsunami.

Another of the scientific revelations at this 2005 conference in England was that the excessive carbon dioxide is not only going up into the atmosphere, it is also seeping into the oceans and killing off the plankton at the bottom of the marine food chain. As a result, all the fish and other forms of marine life will eventually be affected. No one had previously realized that this would be one of the effects of global warming.

If this is the way the human race will die out, then, unlike the dinosaurs during the fifth extinction, we will have a long and painful death, with millions upon millions of environmental refugees involved in the most terrible struggles for food and water. Billions will die. The scale of human suffering is too horrible to contemplate.

So, what is being done about it? What are our world leaders doing?

World leaders have had great difficulty in agreeing upon protocols that will effectively halt this disaster. And even when there have been agreements, they have not always been honored. The net result is that emissions are increasing instead of decreasing. The International Energy Agency now estimates that with the population explosion in developing countries and the rapid industrialization of huge countries like China and India, by 2040 the emissions will have increased by 62 percent!

All the nations of the earth need to cooperate on this one. If a number of nations agree to do what is required while others like the United States and populous "emerging" nations like China and India do not, all of us will perish.

As so many commentators have said, "We know what to do, but we lack the will to do it." Why? Because we do not seem to be able to move beyond our short-sighted selfish interests, our individualism.

Those who have more than enough need to tighten their belts and lower their standard of living. All of us need to give up the idea of unlimited economic growth. But individualism and group selfishness will not allow us to do this. Any politician who proposes anything remotely like this will simply not get the votes of the majority of his or her people. We lack the political will to do what is needed because most people cannot transcend their egos sufficiently to consider the needs of others and especially the needs of future generations. The ego doesn't want to know. So, the problem is denied and knowledge of it is suppressed. That is self-evidently suicidal for the human race.

It is not a matter of blaming all the selfish people in the world for our troubles. It is not appropriate to engage in accusations, condemnations, witch-hunting, or scapegoating. It is a matter of recognizing that we cannot go forward without tackling the problem of unbridled ego—and this includes a good look at our own egos too.

There are many brave activists who spare nothing to raise consciousness and mobilize people to save the earth and there are a growing number of spiritual teachers who work hard to move people beyond the tyranny of the ego. Joanna Macy is surely right when she says, "Something important is happening in our world that you are not going to read about in the newspapers. I consider it the most fascinating and hopeful development of our time, and it is one of the reasons I am so glad to be alive today. It has to do with what is occurring to the notion of the *self.*"[11] Psychologists, philosophers, sociologists, spiritual writers and mystics of different religious traditions are looking at the destructive consequences of selfishness, and at practices— new and old—that might enable us to transcend our narcissism. Most of these studies focus on the ego.

## The Ego and Beyond

Freud, Jung, and other psychologists use the word "ego" in different ways. But the most common use today among psychologists and spiritual writers, and the use that I will make of it, is in reference to the self-centered self, the "I" that imagines itself to be the center of the world, judging everything in terms of how it affects "me" and only "me." The ego is the *selfish self.*

This ego is possessive. It often manifests itself as an insatiable desire for money and possessions. Hence our Western obsession with wealth. Our whole economy is based upon the powerful driving force of self-interest. The unbridled ego wants to control its world: people, events, and nature. Hence the obsession with power and authority.

The ego compares itself with others and competes for praise and privilege, for love, for power and money. This is what makes us envious, jealous, and resentful of others. It is also what makes us hypocrites, two-faced, and dishonest.

This self-centered ego trusts no one outside of itself (unless it has projected its self-centeredness onto someone else). It is this lack of trust that makes us so insecure. We become inevitably full of fears, worries, and anxieties. Our ego or selfish individualism makes us lonely and fearful.

The selfish self loves no one but itself, seeking only its own needs, its own gratification. Totally lacking in compassion or empathy, the ego can be extraordinarily cruel towards others.

What drives us as humans to make others suffer is our loveless egos: our pride and selfishness.

The human ego can also take the form of group selfishness and structures of domination. The lust for power is the ego's attempt to control the world, if necessary at the point of a gun. The lust for money is the expression of the ego's insatiable possessiveness. Institutions and other structures are then set up to pursue these aims. Patriarchy is the social structure that embodies the male ego.

*But*, the ego is not my true self. It is not me. It is a false image of myself. It is the *illusion* that I am a separate, independent, isolated, and autonomous individual. No matter what I imagine myself to be, I am in fact part of an immense universe in which everything is interdependent and intimately interconnected. We are products of evolution, products of our social and cultural upbringing, and products of our psychological conditioning. We do not even begin to become free until we recognize this. When we imagine that as human beings we stand somewhere outside and above the universe looking down upon it, we are not free and independent, we are deluded. It is a case of false consciousness.

All the divisions, conflicts, and rivalries between human beings, and between humans and the rest of nature, arise out of the ego's illusion of separateness and independence.

It seems that in the process of evolution the human species developed the phenomenon we call ego. We developed a self-conscious image of ourselves as separate from the rest of the world. We became self-centered. So, in early infancy, each of us develops something of an ego. The process is called individuation. As we grow up we make use of that ego, but usually in a controlled way in order to accommodate others. The control comes from ourselves or from our culture, religion, or societal laws.

Over the centuries the human ego has been an extraordinarily powerful driving force toward human achievements of all kinds, especially in the West from the time of the Renaissance, the Enlightenment, and the beginnings of science and the Industrial Revolution. It was out of all this that Western individualism developed.

It has often been said that selfishness is natural, and in a sense that is true. But nature is not static; it is evolutionary. The ego has evolved over many thousands of years. Today it has reached a critical point. It has become destructive, so that it would be perfectly natural for us to take a giant leap forward, to transcend the limitations of the ego, to develop a greater, more universal, and more evolved sense of self—not by fighting against anything in us that is natural but by developing another great longing, the natural desire for unity, community, oneness, and love.

CHAPTER 3

# Globalization from Below

Nothing characterizes our experience of life more honestly and comprehensively than our experience of suffering, our own suffering and that of others—together with our habit of making one another suffer. The history of humankind, at least for the period of time for which we have written records, has been a *history of suffering*—as the theologian Johann Metz described it some years ago.

Our history books tell another story. They tell of military victories and conquests, of great civilizations and amazing discoveries and inventions. What they hide or gloss over is the horrific human suffering that accompanied all these events. The underlying suffering of so many millions of people is regarded as of no historical significance. But, as Metz and many others today would point out, what really matters in our history is the suffering of the people.

The history of all our wars is a history of people who were wounded, maimed for life, blown to pieces, melted down by napalm, massacred, tortured, humiliated, and left to die in the trenches. One thinks especially of the women, the children, the elderly, and the bereaved.

The great pyramids of Egypt were built upon the suffering of slaves who died by the thousands. The New World of the Americas was built upon genocide, the wiping out of native American peoples, and the humiliation and agony of African slaves who were forced to row their very confined prison boats across the Atlantic, dropping dead like flies along the way. The real history of the Industrial Revolution is the unwritten story of the pain and deprivation of the workers in the new factories and mines, and of their families. The history of South Africa until recently has been very largely a story of unbearable racial humiliation and hardship.

While in some areas of life there is less suffering today than there was in the past, in other areas there is much more suffering. For example, in some communities these days especially in southern Africa, the HIV/AIDS pandemic causes intolerable suffering, not only for those who are afflicted but also for the millions of terrifyingly traumatized children orphaned by it. What is also worse today is the number of people who live in dire poverty and misery—billions more than in the past. The first obvious consequence of the population explosion is more suffering for more people.

However, what I want to draw attention to as one of the signs of our times is the way in which, in the midst of the most intolerable suffering, we have been moving forward to overcome some of it and hopefully in the future much more of it.

### Structural Change

Suffering in the past (and sometimes in the present too) was made worse by a deep sense of helplessness and powerlessness. It seemed that nothing could be done about it. There was no way out. A measure of relief might come from a caring family or a benevolent dictator, but no real change was possible—in this life.

Some forms of religion offered the consolation of relief and happiness in the next life, but more often than not preachers made the sufferings of people worse by proclaiming that suffering was God's punishment for sin, that it was good for them and that if they did not stop sinning they would spend eternity in excruciating pain, burning in the fires of hell. Worse still was the theology of predestination, which taught that some of us were predestined for hell no matter what we might ever try to do about it.[1]

While this was not the message of all Christian preachers, we should have no illusions about the terrifying reality of human suffering and human cruelty, and about the religious beliefs that presented God as more cruel and sadistic than even the most wicked of human beings.

We have begun to move away from this kind of inhumanity in several ways. One of the most important is our recent history of structural change, or, more specifically, the emergence of the real possibility of changing the structures of power and domination that cause so much suffering in the world.

In the past, feelings of powerlessness and helplessness were based on the assumption that the oppressive structures of societies, cultures, and religions could not be changed.[2] Then came the great revolutions: the French Revolution, the American Revolution, the Russian Revolution, and the numerous revolutions against colonialism and imperialism. These revolutions may not have been very successful. Often the new regimes turned out to be as cruel and oppressive as the structures they were overthrowing. But the revolutions did enable us to discover that *structures of power can be changed.*

In the world of the past, the only change the sufferer could hope for was the change from a cruel king or prince or chief to a more caring one, from a ruthless dictator to a benevolent one. What has developed since then, hesitatingly and not without problems, is the possibility of democratic structures and a belief in human rights. And this has opened the way for the great new phenomenon that we call the struggle for social justice.

This struggle has notched up some remarkable gains over the last two hundred years. One of its first great achievements was the abolition of slavery. New laws made it illegal to buy and sell human beings as pieces of property. In ancient times a structural change like this would have been inconceivable. Even the apostle Paul, who clearly regarded the practice of slavery as contrary to the spirit of Jesus Christ, would have thought of it as a worldly structure that was impossible to change—in this life.

Decolonization too was based upon the conviction that the structures of power could be changed. Colonized peoples struggled for independence and liberation from the great colonizing empires of Spain, Portugal, and Britain, among others.

As far as racism is concerned, we have seen the defeat of the Nazis in Germany, the successes of the civil rights movement in the United States, and, above all, the dismantling of apartheid in South Africa. Struggles against racism continue, but the great racial power structures have been dismantled.

Another truly remarkable change has been the challenge to patriarchy. We have witnessed the worldwide development of women's struggles for equal rights and gender equality in every sphere of life. The struggles continue, but there have been considerable gains since the days when it was thought to be impossible to change the patriarchal structures of power.

## New Voices

The most important result of these and many other liberation struggles has been a breakthrough of new voices onto the scene: the voices of women, black people, indigenous people, workers, peasants, the poor, the untouchables, and even children. In the past these voices were totally suppressed. The suffering of these people could be heard, if at all, only in the voices of their humanitarian sympathizers.

Humanitarian voices have played an important, but limited, role in the struggle against injustice. I am thinking of advocacy groups, non-governmental organizations (NGOs), civil society groups, churches, and other faith-based groups. However, the organization that has contributed most toward humanitarian relief, the protection of human rights, and the securing of international agreements is no doubt the United Nations.

Founded in 1945 to secure peace and cooperation between its member states, the United Nations has often been the voice and the defender of the voiceless. Its various programs promote food security (FAO), assistance for refugees (UNHCR), environmental agreements (UNEP), children's rights (UNICEF), development (UNDP), cooperation in education, science, and culture (UNESCO), and now also the coordination of the struggle against the AIDS pandemic (UNAIDS). The organization's international conferences on women's issues, racism, and the destruction of the environment have provided a basis for the *internationalization* of the struggle for justice.

But now the voice of the voiceless is growing louder each day outside of the United Nations. It is still a muted voice. It still has very little place in the corridors of power and in the mass media, but the gains have been significant. The voice of the voiceless can now be heard in a growing number of people's movements, in publications and international gatherings, and in liberation theologies of various kinds.

In the meantime, the major structures of power continue to re-structure themselves from day to day.


**The Empire**

The overarching inequality today is between the rich and the poor. The structures of power that dominate the human world are making the rich richer and the poor poorer. Billions of people are being marginalized and excluded because there is no place for them in the economy. They are neither producers nor consumers. They are nobodies.

This new form of colonization and imperialism is often called "globalization"—a confusing and ambiguous word that needs to be unpacked. Literally, globalization means "spreading something around the globe." Worldwide diffusion as such is not a problem. Everything depends upon what it is that is being diffused or globalized. The globalization of a deadly disease would constitute a serious problem, but the globalization of an effective vaccine would be good news.

The globalization that many people are protesting about today is the globalization of a particular economic culture, neoliberal capitalism, a thoroughly materialistic worldview based on the principle of the survival of the fittest, a culture that destroys other cultures and indigenous wisdom, making the rich richer and the poor poorer around the world.[3]

While there can be no doubt about the power of the multinational or transnational big corporations in this process of oppressive globalization, their power is limited. It is the power of money. And while in a sense money rules the world, as it has done for thousands of years, the really oppressive power in the human world is the gun. You cannot dominate the world with your money if you do not have the weapons to protect your wealth. Japan is a very rich country, but because it does not have a powerful army and weapons of mass destruction, Japan could not impose its will upon the United States of America, if it ever wanted to do so.

Those who analyze and study the structures of power in the world today are in no doubt about the dominance of the mighty American Empire with its weapons of mass destruction, its armies spread out around the globe (745 bases in 120 countries[4]), its attempts at controlling and dominating every country in the world, its arrogant effort to impose its will upon the whole human world and, through its space programs, on the entire universe. In the final analysis, the globalization we are up against is the globalization of the American Empire.[5]

There is no longer any attempt by the leaders of the United States to disguise their imperial intentions. Today we are simply told that the Empire decides for all of us and that the Empire knows what is best for us and that the highest priority at all times is "American interests." The people of the United States are often as much victims of this power structure as anyone else, even if they do not always see it that way. Moreover, among the Empire's strongest critics and opponents these days one finds citizens of the United States itself.

There are people who imagine that the American Empire will last forever. No empire has ever been able to do that, although I suppose they all thought they were invincible. Apart from the many empires whose rise and fall we read about in the Bible and the famous rise and fall of the Roman Empire, in more recent times we have seen the rise and the fall of the Spanish Empire, the Portuguese Empire, the Japanese Empire, the seemingly unconquerable British Empire, and the mighty Soviet Empire. The seemingly all-powerful American Empire is no exception. Its decline has already begun and that is one of the signs of our times.

### The Empire's Decline and Fall

Sometimes an empire falls because it is conquered by another more powerful one. Sometimes an empire collapses because of its own internal contradictions. Sometimes its decline and fall is a combination of both. I cannot see another military power conquering the United States. But there are growing internal contradictions and there is now another kind of power that is developing extraordinarily quickly and effectively: *the power of peace, compassion, and justice*. It seems to me that there is now a real chance that today's mighty empire might be the last of the great empires and that it will go quickly—as the apartheid regime did in South Africa.

The Empire has become so overconfident, so arrogantly sure of its own righteousness, so blind, so undiplomatic, and so busy with "overkill" that it is unwittingly generating its own opposition, thereby ensuring its own demise—as the apartheid regime did in its final years. Not only has the American Empire given rise to militant Muslim formations and to suicide bombers and other forms of terrorism, but its war on Iraq has created the strongest and largest anti-war peace movement in human history. The anti–Vietnam War peace movement was small and insignificant in comparison. The new peace movement is universal and is destined to become a powerful pressure group.

Closely linked to this is the globalization of compassion for victims—all victims. Until fairly recently, each coherent group (national, cultural, class, ethnic, or religious) felt deeply about the sufferings of its own members but had no feelings at all for the enemy or outsider. This bound groups together and made war and violent conflict possible. It enabled people to suspend all feelings of sympathy toward victims and to unite in an act of violence against anyone who is presented as the scapegoat.[6]

But now an increasing number of people are beginning to experience feelings of compassion for every and any victim, wherever in the world they may be situated.[7] What we should notice in the HIV/AIDS pandemic is not only the unprecedented horrors suffered by people but also the unprecedented upsurge of compassion for victims of the pandemic. The same can be said of the tsunami disaster of December 2004. The response of sympathizers around the world was phenomenal. Most impressive of all, though, with regard to compassion, has been the campaign against poverty that exploded during the middle of 2005. The numbers of people involved in the marches, the cooperation of the churches, the singers who participated in the popular concerts around the world, and the strength of the pressure that was put on the G8 nations all point to a new future for victims of poverty worldwide.

Equally significant have been the peace initiatives of women in war-torn regions around the world. One example would be the meetings between Israeli and Palestinian women.[8] As mothers and wives in the midst of violence, they have much in common. What we are witnessing here is the globalization of compassion and peace. As René Girard says, "Our world did not invent compassion, it is true, but it has universalized it."[9]

## The World Social Forum

Still more powerful and effective is the sudden recognition on the part of almost all involved in struggles for justice in the world today that they are struggling against the same structures of power. Movements and organizations struggling for economic justice, human rights, oppressed minorities, women's rights, and children's rights as well as environmentalists, religious activists, and many others have been coming together on the streets to protest against neo-liberal globalization.

The first of these street protests to hit the headlines took place in Seattle in 1999. Some sixty thousand representatives of a great variety of organizations marched in Seattle where one of the organs of globalization, the World Trade Organization (WTO), was meeting that year. Unfortunately, the demonstration turned violent. It seems that some of the protesters provoked this in order to get media attention. The same thing happened in subsequent years in Prague, Genoa, Davos, Gleneagles, and Hong Kong. There seems to be no end to the globalization of resistance to neo-liberal globalization. In the meantime, suddenly and unexpectedly, a global umbrella body irrupted onto the international scene, the World Social Forum.

The World Social Forum (WSF) is an initiative that came from outside of the United Nations. It includes many of the same movements and organizations that had marched on the streets, but more important, it brings together a large number of people's movements, women's movements, movements of indigenous people and peasant farmers, trade unions, movements against global warming, and AIDS organizations. It is the voice of the silent majority themselves. The Dalits movement, for example, represents the interests of 240 million Indian untouchables. And the large number of women in the WSF, women who represent more than only women's movements, can speak directly or indirectly for half the world's population.

The WSF is not a new international organization. It has no ideology or unifying political theory. It is a *forum* for airing views and experiences—and for listening to one another. The unity of the WSF is not forced, but all who gather under its banner see themselves as part of the struggle against the economic and military globalization of *the Empire*. What is finding a voice in the WSF is the globalization of resistance to the Empire. "Another World Is Possible" is the motto it adopted in 2002.[10]

In reading the political and economic signs of our times, what we notice most of all today is this *globalization from below*. We have noted the globalization of the anti-war and peace movements and the globalization of compassion for all victims. In the World Social Forum we see the globalization of the struggle for justice. It is impossible to predict how and when the American Empire will come to an end, but perhaps in the not too distant future the international groundswell of resistance in the name of peace, compassion, and justice will undermine and dismantle the structures of power and domination.

## CHAPTER 4

# Science after Einstein

For nearly four hundred years Western thinking has been dominated by modern science. For most of this time it has been a major problem for faith. Today this is changing. There is a new science, a new kind of scientific mentality that opens up vast new possibilities for spirituality and faith in God. This change constitutes one of the truly great signs of our times.

## The Scientific Mentality of the Past

The principal architects of the scientific worldview were Francis Bacon (1561–1626), René Descartes (1596–1650), and Isaac Newton (1642–1727). There were others, but these *men* might well be called the *fathers* of modern science.

Science for Bacon was *man's* conquest and taming of nature. Women were seen as part of nature; they could not be counted among the scientific conquerors of nature.

For Descartes, the human body was simply a machine. The rational thinking mind, though, was something completely separate and superior—the ghost in the machine.

Newton saw the whole universe as one gigantic machine. He spoke of it as a clock that had been created by God, wound up, and then left to carry on ticking.

In this worldview, the universe is a collection of objects, the smallest of which are atoms. They operate like the parts of a machine, mechanically and predictably, according to the strict laws of physics, the laws of gravity and motion, and in conformity with the properties God has given each atom. This was a scientific worldview in the sense that it was based upon measurements, controlled experiments and empirical evidence—the "facts" as they appeared to be in those days.

The famous discoveries and inventions of the Industrial Revolution were made possible by this mechanistic worldview. It was Newton's careful study of the laws of gravity and motion that enabled technology to build more and more sophisticated machines.

This seventeenth-century mechanistic worldview became the norm for all scientific endeavors. John Locke saw society as a machine in which the parts were isolated individuals pursuing their own selfish interests and able to cooperate with one another only by means of social contracts. Freud's scientific study of the human psyche and especially of the unconscious mind, brilliant though that study was, was limited by the mechanical and materialistic framework of Freud's thinking. Marx's scientific socialism, based upon his careful analysis of capitalism and his predictions about its future, was deeply influenced by the mechanistic understanding of what "scientific" means. Even Darwin's scientific study of evolution was limited by the view that the only mechanical way in which one species could evolve from another was by natural selection. Western medicine suffered from the same limitation. The body was seen as a kind of sophisticated machine.

In fact, this kind of scientific mentality has influenced the thinking of most of us, especially those who have had a typical Western education in science. There have been and still are exceptions: mystics, poets, artists, some people of faith, those in premodern cultures, and generally, in almost every part of the world, women. In terms of the mechanistic worldview, the thinking of these groups has been regarded as unscientific, superstitious, and magical, but mostly harmless. As the scientists saw it, such irrational ways of thinking contributed nothing to the progress of "mankind."

God was completely absent from this world. If God existed at all, it would have to be in some other spiritual or supernatural world. Hence the two world schizophrenia that most of us grew up with, the dualism that separates the material world from the spiritual world, the body from the soul, creation from the creator.

Then came Albert Einstein (1879–1955).

## The New Science

It is not for nothing that Einstein's name has become a household word for exceptional intelligence. He was a genius like no other. What he and many others during the last hundred years have been able to demonstrate is that the mechanistic worldview that we call science is simply *unscientific*. And while it took some time for the consequences of his discoveries, and other similar discoveries, to be appreciated, today the vast worldwide community of scientists, with few exceptions, has moved beyond the mechanistic view of reality.

What is really significant about this world-shaking paradigm shift is that it is *scientific*. The mechanistic worldview has been dismantled by innumerable experiments, by meticulous measurements, by hard empirical evidence. The mechanical hypothesis can no longer account for the "facts" as scientists know them today.

Although most people have not really caught up with it yet, the new scientific mentality is here to stay. It is the way almost everyone will think in the not too distant future. It will change our consciousness as nothing has ever done before. It stands today as a sign of a very exciting tomorrow.

So, what is this new scientific worldview? We begin with some of the well known discoveries of quantum physics.

## Quantum Physics

One of Einstein's great discoveries was that energy and matter were, in the words of Bill Bryson, "two forms of the same thing: energy is liberated matter; matter is energy waiting to happen."[1] Nor was this some kind of vague theory. Einstein actually measured the amount of matter (its mass) that would be the equivalent of a particular amount of energy. Hence the world's most famous formula: $E=mc^2$.

This could simply not be reconciled with the mechanistic model of physics because energy was supposed to be an activity or movement and matter was supposed to be a thing. How could a thing become a movement and how could an activity become a particle of matter?

But this was just the beginning. Einstein also discovered that light sometimes behaves like a particle and sometimes like a wave. The mechanistic scientists had already decided that light must be a wave and therefore they jumped to the conclusion that there must be some kind of substance in which light waves were moving. They called this hypothetical substance "ether."

Today the scientists tell us that there is no such thing as ether and that light is neither a wave nor a particle. The truth is that our human minds are limited. We cannot understand light; we can only treat it *as if* it were a wave, and for other purposes *as if* it were a particle. In fact it is neither; it is something beyond the human mind and imagination. For us, light is a *mystery*.

Light is a form of energy and energy is of course equally mysterious—although not nearly as mysterious as the atom. When Einstein and numerous other scientists "opened up" the atom and analyzed its "contents" into electrons, protons, neutrons, and numerous other "particles" right down to infinitesimally small quarks, they soon realized that they were not in fact dealing with particles, nor waves, or any other recognizable objects. They were dealing with patterns and relationships. But how can you have patterns and relationships with nothing that is being patterned or related?

The mystery only deepened when the great physicist Niels Bohr came across the quantum leap. Electrons, which we have to treat as particles moving around in an orbit, sometimes *jump* from one orbit to another without passing through the space between the two orbits. How is that possible?

There are any number of other puzzles that defy explanation, not because we do not have enough evidence but because in the subatomic world the empirical evidence is self-contradictory. There seems to be no logic or rationality down there. It is, to us, a very strange world.

The latest theory, or way of describing what appears to be happening in the subatomic world, concerns the quantum vacuum. Ninety percent of any atom is empty space, a vacuum. There is nothing there, not even the hypothetical ether. But electrons and all the other "particles" that seem to be spinning around in the atom emerge out of this nothingness and then disappear again into it. In the words of the mathematical cosmologist, Brian Swimme, "elementary particles crop up out of the vacuum itself—that is the simple and awesome discovery...the base of the universe seethes with creativity."[2] Further on he becomes almost mystical about it: "I use 'all-nourishing abyss' as a way of pointing to this mystery at the base of being."[3]

The quantum physicist who has studied this phenomenon more than most, David Bohm, speaks of the implicate order and the explicate order. The implicate order is the creative vacuum, the universe's unbroken wholeness, which is invisible because it is not available to our senses. The explicate order is the multiplicity and diversity of things and events that arise out of the implicate order and present themselves to us as empirical evidence.[4]

The universe is not what it used to be. It is not a machine. It is a mystery.

### The Universe Is Expanding

Another of Einstein's discoveries was so extraordinary that, for years, he himself could not believe it. His calculations led to the conclusion that the whole universe was either contracting or expanding. That was too much, even for Einstein. But then a few years later the astronomer Edwin Hubble (1889–1953) provided incontrovertible evidence for the phenomenon of a rapidly expanding universe. Before Hubble, the only galaxy we knew about was our own, the Milky Way, and that was not expanding because galaxies are held together by the force of gravity. Today we are aware of something like 140 billion galaxies out there, many of them discovered by Hubble, and they are all moving away from one another in all directions at an ever-increasing speed!

Einstein's calculations had not been mistaken. Years later he spoke of this cover-up of his conclusions as the greatest blunder of his life.

The next step was to read backwards from the present moment to a point in time and space when everything must have started expanding outwards. Known to many as the "Big Bang," it is estimated to have happened between thirteen and fifteen billion years ago.

Some hundreds of thousands of scientists, the best known being Stephen Hawking, then went to work trying to trace the many steps in the evolution of the universe from the first great explosion of pure energy through the development of protons, electrons, atoms, molecules of hydrogen and helium, stars, supernovae (exploding stars), galaxies, planets rotating around stars, and then, on planet Earth, the evolution of life, of which we are an outstanding example. And what a story it has turned out to be.

Much has been written about this unfolding development, but it was Brian Swimme and Thomas Berry who put it all together as one long and exciting story in their book, *The Universe Story: A Celebration of the Unfolding of the Cosmos.* It has become the new creation story that has already fired the imaginations of hundreds of thousands of people. We call it the new cosmology.

After literally millions of experiments and calculations, what we have today is a new worldview that sees our unbelievably vast universe unfolding at an incredible speed from a point smaller than anything we could possibly imagine. And if that does not boggle the mind, we can try to grasp what scientists mean when they tell us that there is no space outside of this universe and no time before the Big Bang, because space and time are created along the way as the universe expands. If you can imagine yourself traveling at some impossible speed toward the edge of the universe, you would eventually find yourself back where you started—because of what Einstein called the curvature of space.

As the biologist J. B. S. Haldane once observed, "The universe is not only queerer than we suppose; it is queerer than we *can* suppose."[5]

## Self-organizing Systems

Biologists have long given up the idea that living organisms are just like machines. Medical practitioners today recognize the ineffectiveness of treating the human body as a separate mechanism. They speak about holistic healing, treating the whole person, and including the person's social and physical environment.

Today living organisms are described as self-regulating systems. They organize themselves, nourish themselves, heal themselves, propagate themselves, protect themselves, and interact creatively with other systems.

We used to call this instinct—in animals if not in plants. Today we talk about genes that have coded messages or instructions that connect with one another in a DNA spiral in the nucleus of every living cell. If we were to write out the instructions contained in any one tiny DNA spiral we would fill about a thousand books of six hundred pages each.

What this means, in the words of Fritjof Capra, is that "the organizing activity of living systems, at any level, is *mental activity*" (emphasis mine).[6] All living things have minds of one kind or another. Mind here is not a thing or an object. It is a particular kind of process. Living and knowing are inseparable.

The human mind, however, is different. Not only is it a more complex process, but, because it is so close to us, it is even more mysterious to us. We call it *consciousness*. Psychologists and mystics have tried to say something about this phenomenon, but it is so basic that it cannot be explained in terms of anything more basic. It has been noted that the most fundamental thing in existence is not matter or atoms or quarks but our own consciousness.

Much study has been done on the phenomenon of consciousness. We can know something consciously or unconsciously. We can become conscious of being conscious. We can become conscious of ourselves as the ones who are conscious (self-consciousness) and it seems that we can experience consciousness as such, with no particular object.[7]

Another interesting way in which the mechanistic worldview is being transcended is through discoveries having to do with chaos theory. It seems that systems of various kinds often exist in a state of chaos or, as they say, "on the edge of chaos," and then suddenly and unpredictably there emerges something called a "strange attractor" that rearranges the chaos into some new order.

Predictability had been the cornerstone of Newtonian physics and of the great advances in technology. This is still true at some levels, but not always and everywhere, it seems. Scientists are discovering more and more events that could never have been predicted. The mystery deepens.

## Holons

Science and philosophy had always operated on what is called linear causality: A causes B causes C and so forth. But if one just thinks about it, any particular event has multiple causes, conditions, and influences, not to mention the reactions we call feedback. One has only to think of the role of temperature, pressure, the ecosystem, and other surrounding events to realize that there is no possible line of causality that is independent and disconnected from everything else that is going on. There is always a whole web of causes and conditions, and each one of these causes and conditions is the result of a further web of causes and conditions until the whole universe since the beginning of time is seen as in some way involved in any particular event! Everything—without exception—is connected to everything else.

The universe is not a collection of objects; it is a system of systems within systems. This applies to more than just living organisms. Every natural thing is a system and part of a system, a whole and a part of a greater whole. "Holon" is the word that has been coined for this.

Perhaps the final nail in the coffin of the mechanistic worldview was the discovery that the whole, any whole, is greater than its parts, and that it is the whole that determines how the parts will behave. A machine like a clock or a car or a jet plane is not a whole. It is nothing more than the sum total of its parts working together. But natural wholes from living organisms to ecosystems to galaxies operate differently. Each of them is more than the sum total of its parts.

This is why some scientists today speak of the earth as Gaia. It is not a living organism like a plant. It does not reproduce itself, but it does seem to be self-regulating. In some mysterious way the earth as a whole, as a "self," regulates the temperature, the impact of the sun's rays, and so forth in order to survive and to continue to evolve.

## Science and Religion

This is the scientific thinking of the future, and already it is revolutionizing the relationship between science and religion. This is going to make an enormous difference to any genuine search for God today and tomorrow. Suddenly, from being an obstacle, science has become an aid, a kind of springboard into spirituality and mysticism. This is not because science can *prove* anything about God or faith. Rather, science has now recognized its own limitations. Today it is the scientists who are saying: "We don't know and for the most part we can never know. It is a mystery."

On the other hand, religion, spirituality, and mysticism will also be revolutionized by this new scientific mentality. For example, there is only one world, one universe. It is no longer possible to think of God, the human soul, and other spirits as inhabitants of another world. Moreover, the universe is one interconnected whole. We are not separate and independent parts. There is an unimaginable number of diverse species and systems, but together they form one whole. And, most important of all, we humans are not in control of the universe.

## The Signs in Summary

Looking at the signs as a whole and together, I am reminded of the famous quote from Charles Dickens' *A Tale of Two Cities*: "It was the best of times, it was the worst of times." The signs of our times are strikingly ambiguous and confusing. We have moved into an age that is full of promise but fraught with unimaginable dangers. Nor are we all in the same place. Some have moved far forward, others are moving backwards, and still others have no idea where they are going—which makes it very difficult to sum up where we are as a human family at this moment in our evolution. A metaphor may help.

We are like a giant ocean liner that has come loose from it moorings and is drifting out to sea. The dangers ahead are incalculable. Are we heading for shipwreck and extinction? Some want to return to the safety of the harbor, but that is no longer possible. Others are so distracted that they are not aware of the fact that we are drifting. Still others would like to jump ship and swim to the shore alone. But we are now too far out and there is no longer any possibility of going it alone. We are all in this boat together.

On the other hand, a growing number of passengers view this drifting out to sea as a unprecedented opportunity to move away from the slavery and suffering of the past, to search for the promised land of freedom and happiness. New possibilities are opening up on the horizon every day. The hunger for a new spirituality is hopeful. The desire for justice, peace, and cooperation is encouraging. The new voices from below and the globalization of compassion for those in need are promising. The dangers of individualism are being recognized. And the new science provides us with a map of where we are, where we have come from, and where we might be going.

The dangers and threats remain. The ship is already leaking, and while some are trying to repair the leak, others in their selfish blindness are creating new leaks and ignoring the icebergs ahead of us. There is no storm at sea. Nature is not hostile to us. The storm is on board between the passengers themselves—each blindly pursuing his or her own agenda.

But who is steering this ship? Who is in control? Market forces? The military? The great American Empire? Pure chance? Or God?

It is in this context, at this moment in the evolution of our universe, that we are invited to consider anew and to take seriously the spiritual wisdom of Jesus of Nazareth.

# II

# JESUS' SPIRITUALITY

Our primary concern in these three chapters will not be Jesus' life, his story—nor even his teachings. Our primary concern will be his spirituality. He does not seem to have spoken much about his own spiritual life, but, as I pointed out in the introduction, by reading between the lines we can extrapolate some of the elements of what must have been an extraordinarily profound spirituality. We will have to look at what Jesus did and said and taught, but only in order to appreciate the spirituality that must have been behind his activities and teachings. What was the secret of his extraordinary life—and death? What did he feel strongly about? What was so memorable about him? What made him so deeply loved and admired by some and hated by others?

This is not as impossible a task as it may at first sight appear to be. Despite the fact that Jesus did not write anything himself, we have an enormous amount of information about Jesus, about the times in which he lived, and about the impression he made upon people. No set of books has been studied as thoroughly and meticulously as the gospels, and no historical person has received anything like the attention he has. We will draw on some of this scholarship and more especially on the experience of those who have taken him seriously and walked in his footsteps: the saints and mystics.

Jesus lived in a world that was very different from ours. Our postmodernism, our science and technology, our individualism, our globalization, our destruction of the earth, and our alienation from nature have generated a great gulf between ourselves and the people of first-century Palestine. One of the principal differences is that Jesus and his Jewish contemporaries took it for granted that God was a person. Today we can no longer take that for granted. Many people have difficulty with the idea of a personal God—and not without reason. We will discuss this in chapters 13 and 16. In these earlier chapters we will speak of Jesus' very personal God without explanation or apology. Our day and age has much to learn from Jesus in this respect too.

## CHAPTER 5

# A Revolution

Jesus was a Jewish peasant. His spirituality would have found its original inspiration in the Hebrew Scriptures. The world he lived in was Jewish, although that does not mean it was faithful to the best in the Hebrew Scriptures. We cannot assume that everything we find in the Hebrew Scriptures was understood and practiced in first-century Palestine, any more than societies or institutions that call themselves Christian today can be assumed to be living out the Sermon on the Mount.

Apart from anything else, the Hebrew Bible encompasses a great variety of worldviews and spiritualities spread over a long period of time. In Jesus' time, as in other times, there were differences of interpretation, different ideas about what it meant to be Jewish, and a range of "human traditions" as Jesus would call them (Mk 7:8,13).

It was a Jewish world, but we should not underestimate the growing influence of Greek culture emanating from the surrounding Greek cities. More important still was the globalization of the Roman Empire that was having an ever increasing influence on the life of the people. The lifestyle and values of the Greco-Roman world were being adopted by the rich and the powerful: the Herods, the chief priests, the elders (nobility), and the rich landowners. Most of them lived lives of luxury and decadence.[1]

All these things characterized the world that Jesus turned upside down. His life, his message, and his spirituality were in that sense revolutionary. Jesus was not a reformer. He did not propose a number of improvements to the religious beliefs and practices of his time—like patching up an old garment. He turned the world, both Jewish and Gentile, upside down. This does not mean that Jesus was a typical revolutionary in the political sense of the word. He did not simply want to replace those presently in power with others who were not yet in power. He was looking at something more radical than that. He took the values of his time, in all their variety, and turned them on their heads. He was busy with a *social* revolution, rather than a *political* one,[2] a social revolution that called for a deep spiritual conversion.

A social revolution is one that turns the social relations between people in a society upside down. A political revolution is one that changes the power relations in a society by overthrowing one government and replacing it with another. Jesus, like most other oppressed Jews in his time, was hoping for political liberation from Roman oppression. But he saw himself as a prophet whose immediate mission was the introduction of a social and spiritual revolution. The dismantling of the structures of power would follow later.

## Turning the World Upside Down

Jesus' sayings, especially those that were collected into the Sermon on the Mount, were subversive of almost everything his contemporaries took for granted. He spoke of turning the other cheek instead of taking revenge, of loving one's enemies instead of hating them, of doing good to those who hate you, of blessing those who curse you, and of forgiving them all seventy times seven times (Mt 5:38-43; Lk 6:27-37; Mt 18:22).

That alone would have revolutionized social relationships among the peasants he preached to as well as the relationships between different groups and classes, and between religions and nations. But it did not end there. Even more revolutionary was what he had to say about the rich and the poor.

The assumption was that God had blessed the rich with wealth and that they were the fortunate ones. Jesus stood up and proclaimed the very opposite. "Blessed are you who are poor" (Lk 6:20). In other words, it is not the rich who are blessed or fortunate, but the poor. This does not mean that it is good to be destitute and in need. Nor is it a promise that one day the poor will be rich. It means, "You should regard yourselves as fortunate that you are not among the rich and the wealthy." It is those who are rich who are the unfortunate ones: "Woe to you who are rich" (Lk 6:24). It is they who should be pitied because it is they who are going to find it very difficult to live in the world of the future (the kingdom of God) where everything will be shared.[3] The rich will find it very difficult to share. They will be like camels trying to get through the eye of a needle. The poor are fortunate because they will find it easy to share.

To appreciate something of the impact that such a reversal must have had, we might imagine someone who goes around today telling the rich and those who have a high standard of living that they are not blessed, that in fact they are most unfortunate. Why? Because the only way the human race can survive will be for the rich to lower their standard of living and share their wealth with others. The rich are going to find that very difficult.

In similar vein, Jesus says that if people hate you, exclude you, revile you, and defame you, you should rejoice because that is how they always treat prophets. It is when they speak well of you that you can count yourself unfortunate (Lk 6:22, 23, 26). In other words, forget about your reputation. When people criticize you and discredit you, it may be a blessing in disguise.

## Equal Dignity

Jesus was uncompromising in his belief that all human beings were equal in dignity and worth. He treated the blind, the
lame and the cripple, the outcasts and beggars with as much respect as that given to those of high rank and status.[4] He refused
to consider women and children unimportant or inferior. This
turned a carefully ordered society of status and honor upside
down—even more so when he advocated moving down the social ladder instead of striving to reach the top. He taught his
followers to take the lowest place, so that when they argued
among themselves about who was the greatest, he showed
them a little child, a person who had no rank or status at all in
that society, and told them to strive to be like children (Mk
9:33–37 parr).

Among other things, this approach pulls down from their
thrones "the learned and the wise." They have no monopoly on
the truth. In fact, their wisdom and learning can blind them to the
truth. Often enough the simple and uneducated little child is
wiser than those who are learned. "I thank you, Father," Jesus
says, "for revealing these things not to the learned and the wise
but to mere infants" (Lk 10:21 par; my translation).

Among those who would have been regarded as mere children in terms of status and learning at the time of Jesus, and
who would therefore have appreciated his message, were
*women*. One of the ways in which Jesus turned his world upside down was by giving women exactly the same value and
dignity as men. He stood out among his contemporaries as the
only teacher who could count women among his friends and
disciples. We hear of Mary of Bethany whom he encouraged to
sit at his feet as a disciple (Lk 10:38-42). Even more controver-
sial was his close friendship with Mary Magdalene, whom he
taught and with whom he seems to have discussed many
things.[5] His mixing so freely with women, especially those who

were known as prostitutes, was nothing less than a scandal (Lk 7:39; Mt 11:19). The one thing Jesus was not concerned about was his reputation.

What he was concerned about was the way prostitutes and women caught in adultery were treated in that society. They, and not the men, were blamed and condemned as sinners. Prostitution and adultery are not possible without men who make the demands and provide the money. Why do the women always get the blame? Jesus' position is beautifully illustrated in the story of his rescuing the woman accused of adultery from the men who wanted to stone her (Jn 8:1-11).[6]

## Subversive Stories

In his booklet on the theology of story, John Dominic Crossan has argued that, while a *myth* is a story that confirms the status quo and reconciles its apparent contradictions, a *parable* is a story that undermines the status quo and reveals its contradictions.[7]

The subversiveness of a statement like: "Those who exalt themselves will be humbled and those who humble themselves will be exalted" (Lk 14:11; 18:14; Mt 23:12), is brought home to us in the parable of the Pharisee and the tax collector who go up to the temple to pray (Lk 18:9-14).

In Jesus' time, the scribes and the Pharisees were held in high regard. With the chief priests and elders they were the religious leaders who knew what was pleasing to God and what was not pleasing to God. The tax collectors, on the other hand, were universally hated and treated as outcasts in that society. The tax system was grossly unjust. The poor were mercilessly bled by a triple tax: the Roman tax, Herod's tax, and the temple tax. But it was those who were employed to collect the taxes who had to face the anger and rejection of the people. They no doubt often exploited the situation for their own benefit. Jesus, however, had some sympathy and understanding for these men who, like the prostitutes, always got the blame. Against everyone's expectations he chose to stay at the house of Jericho's infamous tax collector, Zacchaeus (Lk 19:1-10).

In the parable all expectations are reversed. The Pharisee, because he is proud and boastful, is not justified in the eyes of God: "God, I thank you that I am not like other people." The tax collector, on the other hand, because he humbles himself, *is* justified in the eyes of God.

While everyone assumed that religious leaders like the scribes and the Pharisees, the chief priests and the elders, would be the first to be accepted into the kingdom of God, Jesus dared to stand up and say that the prostitutes and tax collectors would be entering God's new world ahead of the religious leaders (Mt 21:31). That must have upset the assumptions of almost everyone, including the prostitutes and tax collectors themselves. "The first will be last and the last will be first" (Mk 10:31).

The story of the Samaritan who helps a robbed and injured Jew, while a Jewish priest and Levite walk by on the other side (Lk 10:30-37), subverts all the myths about Jews and Samaritans. Samaritans were thought to be half-pagan heretics. Jesus is saying to his fellow Jews not only that they should include the hated Samaritans in their love of neighbor but also that they might even learn something from a Samaritan about loving one's neighbor.

To appreciate the impact this story must have had on Jesus' contemporaries, we might retell it as the story of an injured Christian soldier who is helped by a Muslim fundamentalist while a Christian military chaplain and a Christian social worker walk by on the other side. Impossible? Why? The significance of Jesus' parables even for today is that they shock us out of our prejudices.

In the parable of the workers in the vineyard (Mt 20:1-16), Jesus turns the accepted understanding of *justice* upside down.

When the employer pays those who worked in the vineyard for one hour as much as he pays those who worked all day, is he not guilty of an injustice? Jesus says no. The employer paid those who worked through the heat of the day the wage that was agreed upon. One denarius is in fact a very generous wage for a day's work. When these workers complain, it is not because an injustice has been done to them; it is because the employer has been generous to others. In other words, it is not a matter of justice but of *envy*. The employer chose to pay those who worked for only a short time the same wage because their needs and the needs of their families would have been the same.

In the parable of the prodigal son (Lk 15:11-32), the elder brother feels that he has been treated unjustly. He has always done what is right, so why should there be a celebration for his recklessly wasteful and depraved brother instead of himself? But, as Jesus sees it, the older brother has not been treated unjustly; he is simply *jealous*. He wants to be preferred. He wants to see his brother punished, not forgiven.

## Relativizing the Law

The spirituality of Jesus' time was based upon the law, the Torah. Jesus turned that on its head too—not by rejecting the law but by relativizing it. "The Sabbath was made for humankind, and not humankind for the Sabbath," he says (Mk 2:27). In other words, the Sabbath laws, and by implication all God's laws, are intended to be of service to us as human beings. We do not exist in order to serve or worship the law. That would be idolatry.

Jesus felt perfectly free, therefore, to break the law whenever observing it would do harm to people, because doing harm to people was never the intention of the law. His behavior, however, was regarded as irredeemably scandalous, especially when he taught his followers to do the same (Mt 12:1-5).

In the religious culture of the time, the law was not only the ten commandments but also the comprehensive system of ritual purity and cleanliness that we known as the Holiness Code. Everything—time, space, people, things, and food—was ordered and arranged according to greater and lesser degrees of holiness or purity.[8]

Jesus saw all the laws of ritual purity as human traditions that distorted the intentions of God's law (Mt 15:1-20 par). "It is not what goes into the mouth that defiles a person, but it is what comes out of the mouth that defiles" (Mt 15:11). He not only ignored the distinction between clean and unclean food and the ritual washing of hands before eating, but he touched corpses and lepers and women who were menstruating—all things that were taboo in terms of the Holiness Code.

What mattered for Jesus was people and their needs. Everything else was relative to that.

## The Upside-down Kingdom

Jesus lived at a time when the Jewish people were on "high alert" awaiting the imminent arrival of a Messiah who would restore the long-awaited kingdom or reign of God. Expectations about what, when, where, and how varied enormously. Speculation was rife. Would there be some miraculous divine intervention? Would the Romans be defeated? Would the Messiah-king march triumphantly into Jerusalem with an army? Or would it all happen in some other way?

The Essenes had gone into the desert to purify themselves in preparation for the event. John the Baptist was expecting God's judgment to descend upon Israel itself. Ordinary, simple people were waiting and praying for the liberation of Jerusalem from the Romans (Lk 1:68, 71, 74; 2:25, 38). At the end of

Luke's gospel, the two disciples on the road to Emmaus say that they had hoped that Jesus would have been the one to liberate Israel (Lk 24:21).

Jesus turned these expectations upside down. He had a quite different idea of what the reign of God on earth might mean, and the fundamental reason for this was that he saw God differently. God was not like some great emperor, not like those who lord it over people and make their authority felt (Mk 10:42 par). God was not even like some benevolent dictator. Jesus had come to experience God as a loving Father, his *abba*. Consequently, Jesus saw God's reign as more like the "reign" of the loving father in the parable who forgives his prodigal son unconditionally, who rejoices at the return of his lost child, who gives no thought to punishment or retribution, who does not want to hear anything about his son's debauchery and waste of money. All he wants to do is celebrate with his family (Lk 15:11-32).

The community or society Jesus hoped for was more like a *family* of brothers and sisters with God as their loving parent.[9] His image of God's kingdom or domain was of a happy, loving household rather than a conquering, oppressive empire.

The reign of God would thus not come down from above; it would rise up from below, from the poor, the little ones, the sinners, the outcasts, the lost, from the villages of Galilee.[10] They would become like brothers and sisters who care for one another, identify with one another, protect one another, and share with one another.

This is not to suggest that Jesus' attitude to the family was in any way conventional. He turned that upside down too. What could be more shocking than his statement: "If anyone comes to me without *hating* his father, mother, wife, children, brothers, sisters, yes and his own life too, he cannot be my disciple" (Lk 14:26; my translation). Of course what he meant was "without *not-preferring*."[11] In other words, one cannot be a member of God's family-like kingdom if one still gives preference to one's conventional family.

We see Jesus doing precisely that—not giving preference to his own family. When he is informed that his mother and brothers have come looking for him, he replies:

"Who are my mother and my brothers?" And looking at those who sat around him he said, "Here are my mother and my brothers! Whoever does the will of God is my brother and sister and mother." (Mk 3:33-35)

He sees his own mother as blessed, not because she is his biological mother, but because she "hears the word of God and keeps it" (Lk 11:27-28; my translation). Jesus wants to move beyond the limitations of the blood family or family of close relatives to the broader family of God's kingdom. An exclusive love for one's close family would be a form of group selfishness.

This does not mean that Jesus sees the new family-like kingdom as the whole human race. We must love all human beings, even our enemies, and treat them all as our brothers and sisters, but the new community is the family of those who *love one another*. If your enemy continues to hate you and curse you, that person continues to exclude himself or herself from God's new family. In fact, members of your own blood family could turn against you and reject you despite your love for them. That is why Jesus can foresee that the formation of a new family of God might divide and cause conflict within our narrow, conventional families (Lk 12:51-53 par).

Like all families, God's family will meet around a table for meals. Hence the centrality of meals in Jesus' life, his "table fellowship" as it is sometimes called. What also follows is the sharing that is characteristic of family life. We see this in the common purse of Jesus and his disciples, and later in the first community in Jerusalem (Acts 2:44-45; 4:32-37). It was this understanding of the kingdom as family that led the first Christians to address one another as brother and sister, something that no other religious group of the time would have done.[12] Moreover these first Christians, it seems, would greet one another with a kiss on the lips, which in those days only members of the same family would have done.[13]

It is with this understanding of what God's reign on earth might mean that Jesus begins to speak about it as not an exclusively future event that we must sit back and wait for. God's kingdom is a present reality. It has already arrived among us. We don't have to wait for signs and portents (Mt 12:38-39 par). We can detect the finger of God in what is already happening (Lk 11:20). God's community or family is like the leaven or yeast already at work in the world (Mt 13:33 par). It is a mustard seed that will grow into something much bigger (Mk 4:31-32 parr).

Here again, Jesus has turned the expectations of his contemporaries upside down. What we are waiting for is already here. That does not mean that we should give up hoping for a better world. But it is important to realize that the seed or embryo of that future world is already in our midst.[14]

## The Upside-down Messiah

It was with extreme reluctance that Jesus allowed himself to be spoken of as the Messiah. He discouraged his disciples from saying this to people because he was not a Messiah in the sense in which most of them understood that word (Mt 16:20 parr). He had no intention of being served by the people, nor did he want his disciples to be like rulers who are served by others. He wanted to be the servant (Mk 10:42-45 parr). It is hard to imagine how strange this reversal of the relationship between master and servant must have sounded to the ears of his contemporaries. John the evangelist captures it powerfully with his story of Jesus washing his disciples' feet (Jn 13:4-16).

Jesus did not try to avoid the crucially important role that he had been called to play. He would preach, teach, and introduce the kingdom or family of God, but he would have to do so by suffering and dying for it. His image of the true Messiah would be that of the suffering servant as depicted in the Book of Isaiah (Is 52:13–53:12).

This would be the most radical reversal of all. Jesus was not going to be the triumphant conquering Messiah who would crush and kill Israel's oppressors, humiliating them and making them into victims in order to liberate his people. He would triumph by being conquered, by being arrested, beaten, humiliated, and nailed to a cross like a rebellious slave or a common criminal—the most disgraceful and shameful death imaginable in those days.

He was not the *victor*; he was the *victim*. And, paradoxically, this would turn out to be his greatest achievement. Truth and justice were on the side of the victim. In fact, that is where God is to be found—on the side of the world's victims. This is what Jesus had been saying all along.

René Girard sees the reversal of victim and victor as the final answer to the problem of violence. Instead of sacrificing someone or other as a scapegoat to save the people, Jesus takes upon himself the role of scapegoat or sacrificial lamb.[15]

From the point of view of the world around him, *Jesus was a failure*. They arrested him, charged him, and executed him for treason. Nothing turned the world of his time upside down more radically than treating this kind of failure as a success. It was his willingness to fail that revolutionized the spirituality of the time. His death was his triumph.

Jesus' willingness to die for others meant that he was alive and his executioners were dead. This excruciating paradox was a very important part of his spirituality. He expressed it as a riddle or paradox about life and death that appears in a variety of forms in all the gospels. It can be summed up as:

Anyone who saves his/her life will lose it.
Anyone who loses his/her life will save it.[16]

Nothing contradicts the conventional attitude with regard to ego more thoroughly than this. When we are unwilling to give up our lives for others, we are already dead. When we are willing to die for others, we are truly alive. Or, when we are unwilling to let go of our egos, we are dead. When we are willing to let go, we begin to live with an abundance of life. That is why, shortly after his crucifixion, Mary Magdalene and then the other disciples experienced Jesus as very much alive—as risen from the dead.

## Right Side Up

I have been describing Jesus' radical criticism as turning the world *upside down*. A more accurate way of describing it would be to say that Jesus was turning the world *right side up*. What Jesus was drawing attention to was a world without all the distortions and illusions of the ego: pride, envy, jealousy, self-centeredness, self-importance, lovelessness, and isolation from one another—as individuals and as groups.

Jesus spoke of this right-side-up world as God's world, as the emerging kingdom or family of God. In fact, what Jesus was pointing to was *the real world*. Our conventional wisdom is that unselfish, egoless love is unnatural and that it is self-interest that keeps the economy going and motivates people to accomplish great things. But for Jesus that is not the real world; it is an upside-down world that needs to be turned right side up.

The real world that he uncovered would have appeared to many of his contemporaries to be impractical, foolish, and lacking the approval of legitimate authority. Paul describes it as the paradoxical wisdom of God:

Jews demand signs and Greeks desire wisdom, but we proclaim Christ crucified, a stumbling block to Jews and foolishness to Gentiles. . . . For God's foolishness is wiser than human wisdom. (1 Cor 1:22-23, 25)

Jesus irrupted onto the scene in Palestine at that time with a new consciousness, a wisdom that the scriptures would call the wisdom of God. But where did this man from Nazareth get this wisdom?

# CHAPTER 6

# A Prophet and a Mystic

In their speculations about who Jesus was, his contemporaries agreed that, whatever else, he was a prophet (Mk 8:27-28 parr; Lk 7:16). Some might have thought that he was a false prophet, but he clearly spoke and acted like a prophet. And that is surely how Jesus saw himself (Lk 4:24). He does not seem to have ever contradicted anyone who referred to him as a prophet. In its basic inspiration, therefore, Jesus' spirituality was like that of the Hebrew prophets.

## Speaking Out

Prophets are people who speak out when others remain silent. They criticize their own society, their own country, or their own religious institutions. Those who criticize hostile nations or foreign religions are not called prophets. True prophets are men and women who stand up and speak out about the practices of their own people and their own leaders—while others remain silent.

This leads inevitably to tension and even some measure of conflict between the prophet and the establishment. In the Hebrew Scriptures we see how the prophets clashed with kings and sometimes priests too. Jesus was painfully aware of this tension or conflict in the traditions of the prophets. "Blessed are you when people hate you, and when they exclude you, revile you, and defame you...for that is what their ancestors did to the prophets" (Lk 6:22, 23 par). Jesus saw those who killed the prophets in the past as the ancestors or predecessors of the scribes and Pharisees (Mt 23:29-35).

The tension or conflict is between authority and experience. True prophets are not part of the authority structure of their society or their religious institution. Unlike priests and kings, prophets are never appointed, ordained, or anointed by the religious establishment. They experience a special calling that comes directly from God, and their message comes from their experience of God: "Thus says the Lord God."

We have seen how boldly and radically Jesus spoke out against the assumptions and practices of the social and religious establishment of his time. He turned their world upside down. The conflict that this created became so intense that in the end they killed him to keep him quiet.

Any attempt to practice the same spirituality as Jesus would entail learning to speak out boldly as he did—and facing the consequences.


**Reading the Signs**

Prophets are typically people who can foretell the future, not as fortune-tellers, but as people who have learned to read the signs of their times. It is by focusing their attention on, and becoming fully aware of, the political, social, economic, military, and religious tendencies of their time that prophets are able to see where it is all heading.

Reading the signs of his times would have been an integral part of Jesus' spirituality.

In the first place, like many of the Hebrew prophets, Jesus must have seen the threatening armies of a powerful empire on the horizon—in this case the Roman Empire. Imperial power was well known to the prophets. At one time or another the people of Israel had been oppressed by the Egyptians, the Canaanites, the Assyrians, the Babylonians, the Persians, and the Greeks. The prophets warned against collaborating with these power structures and promised that each of them would one day decline and fall—which they did. In this the prophets saw the finger of God.

In Jesus' view, it would only be a matter of time before the Roman armies felt sufficiently provoked to attack and destroy Jerusalem. "When you see Jerusalem surrounded by armies, then know that its desolation has come near" (Lk 21:20). "Indeed the days will come upon you, when your enemies will set up ramparts around you and surround you, and hem you in on every side. They will crush you to the ground, you and your children within you, and they will not leave within you one stone upon another" (Lk 19:43-44 ).

For most Jews, the destruction of the temple in Jerusalem would mean the destruction of their worship, their culture, and their nation. Jesus' concern was not for the future of the temple but for the people of Jerusalem, especially the women and children who would suffer so much at the hands of the Romans (Lk 19:44; 21:21-24). But Jesus knew, as the Hebrew prophets had known, that all empires come and go. "Jerusalem will be trampled on by the Gentiles [Romans], until the times of the Gentiles are fulfilled" (Lk 21:24).[1]

What Jesus must also have seen was the spiral of violence in which the Galilean peasants were caught up. Recent studies have made us aware of the peasant society in which Jesus lived and of the fact that Jesus himself would have been indeed a peasant. Artisans like carpenters and fishermen were also peasants.[2] Peasants were not only poor, they were exploited and oppressed—and not only by the Romans, but also by the Herods and the rich landowners. They were so heavily taxed that they almost inevitably ended up in debt. As their plight continued to worsen, what developed was a spiral of violence.[3] Peasants and artisans would try to resist their exploitation. The result would be violent repression, which in turn would lead to revolt, giving rise to even more repression.

Jesus, reading the signs of the times from the perspective of a Galilean peasant, would have seen that this spiral of violence held no hope for the poor and the oppressed. The people were powerless and helpless. Was it in reference to the peasants of Galilee that we are told that he saw the crowds as "harassed and helpless, like sheep without a shepherd" (Mt 9:36)?

The experience of insecurity led to an upsurge in religious fervor: new movements, new sects, and new ideas. The people were desperate to know what God was going to do and what God wanted them to do. While this was not quite the same as today's hunger for spirituality, it was a desperate search for God.

Observing the pain and suffering of the peasants and other poor people who were becoming poorer every day and crying out for their daily bread, shocked by the hypocrisy and self-righteousness of so many religious leaders, moved by the "lostness" and brokenness of many sincere people, Jesus seems to have decided that what the people needed was healing. And there were signs that this was already taking place.

When John the Baptist's disciples ask Jesus what is happening, he says:

> Go and tell John what you hear and see: the blind receive their sight, the lame walk, the lepers are cleansed, the deaf hear, the dead are raised, and the poor have good news brought to them. (Mt 11:4-5)

The successful work of healing among the poor and the encouraging news of God's love that Jesus himself brings to the peasants and beggars is the outstanding sign that something new is being born. It is what was foretold by Isaiah (29:18-19; 35:5-6; 61:1-2) and it augurs well for the future. Nor is it only Jesus who is doing this. His disciples as well as others from outside their circle are also busy with this great work (Lk 9:49-50 par).

In these hopeful signs, and possibly many others, Jesus sees the finger of God. And if it is indeed the Work of God, "then the kingdom of God has come to you" (Lk 11:20 par). In other words, God's reign has begun.

## God's Messenger

Jesus spoke, as most prophets do, for or on behalf of God. In fact he seems to have done so more confidently and boldly than any other prophet. He does not preface his message with words like: "The Lord God says." He simply announces his message with: "But I say to you."

Where did Jesus derive this unshakeable assurance that he could speak so directly for God? "Where did this man get this wisdom?" his contemporaries ask (Mt 13:54). After all, Jesus is just a peasant from an unimportant Galilean village called Nazareth.

Prophets experience not only a special calling from God, but also a special closeness to God that enables them to understand God's "feelings" and "thoughts" about what is happening or will happen in the future.[4] It is this mystical experience of union with God that enables them to speak on God's behalf.

In reading the gospels, the general impression we get is that Jesus was very much a man of action: preaching, teaching, healing, and confronting the religious and political leadership. What we do not always notice is that behind, and in support of, all these activities was a life of constant prayer and profound contemplation.

One of the most consistent memories his disciples seem to have had of Jesus was of a person who was frequently wrapped in prayer. They often saw him praying. Sometimes he would just move a short distance away from them to pray (Mt 26:36;

Lk 22:41; 11:1). They said that once while he was praying they saw his appearance change and his face shine (Mt 17:2 parr).

Jesus seems to have taken every possible opportunity of getting away to a quiet and lonely place for prayer and reflection. "In the morning, while it was still very dark," Mark tells us, "he got up and went out to a deserted place, and there he prayed" (1:35 see also 6:46 and Lk 4:42). Luke says he did this regularly (5:16). Before choosing his twelve apostles, he spent the whole night in prayer, we are told (Lk 6:12). He recommended prayer in the privacy of one's room, because he had no time for those who "love to stand and pray in the synagogues and at the street corners, so that they may be seen by others" (Mt 6:5-6). He called such people hypocrites. We can be sure that he spent much time praying behind closed doors.

## The Contemplative Years

Jesus was first and foremost a contemplative. His busy public life seems to have started at about the age of thirty, and to have lasted for no more than three years. The period before this is referred to as his "hidden" life. Hidden or not, I am sure that it was filled with prayer, contemplation, and agonizing discernment. How else would he have been able to act with such clarity and confidence during his short public life? He was fully human and therefore had to grow and develop over time like any other human being. As Luke puts it, "Jesus grew in wisdom and in stature" (Lk 2:52 NIV; see also Lk 2:40).

At some stage he must have learnt to read and write—in the synagogue, no doubt. Luke has him listening to the learned theologians of the time, the scribes, and asking them questions in the temple (Lk 2:41-50). In one way or another he must have spent years, many years, grappling with the meaning of the scriptures, with the signs of the times, and with what he himself might be called to be and to do.

One particularly important experience of God's love and God's call happened while he was at prayer after his baptism in the Jordan (Lk 3:21-22 parr). He felt that the Spirit of God had descended upon him like a dove and that he had been chosen to be a prophet or servant or son of God in some very special way.

We are told that Jesus spent forty days in the desert. The number forty is thematic. It echoes the Hebrew slaves' forty years in the desert. So perhaps Jesus spent even more than forty days in a deserted place. Whatever the case may be, he seems to have spoken of this period as a time of temptation when he struggled with God's will and the very nature of his calling (Lk 4:1-13; Mt 4:1-11).[5] Was he to spend his life finding bread to feed the hungry (turning stones into bread)? Was he to take power and rule over Israel and the kingdoms of the world (as Satan promised)? Was he to do something sensational like jumping off the pinnacle of the temple to attract attention (hoping the angels would catch him)?

Can we see here Jesus' own struggle with his ego? The ego, as we have seen, is a false image of ourselves that we can identify with or reject as a temptation. Could Satan be the premodern way of thinking about what we today call our ego?

We can also surmise that during these more contemplative years Jesus was busy reading the signs of his times. As I pointed out in *Jesus Before Christianity,* when Herod arrested John the Baptist, Jesus left the desert and the river Jordan, gave up baptizing people, and started a dramatically new ministry of preaching and healing in Galilee—focusing on the poor, the sinners, and the sick, the lost sheep of the house of Israel.[6] Was this not the result of a contemplative re-interpretation of the signs of his times? What had now dawned was a new time, quite different from the time of John the Baptist.[7]

In any case, Jesus' union with God was something he became more deeply conscious of as he grew in wisdom and stature over the years before beginning his public life. And while it would obviously not be possible for us to reconstruct this development of consciousness, there are some clues as to what his contemplative prayer and mysticism might have meant.

## Jesus' Mysticism

Jesus was a mystic. "Mystics" and "mysticism" are not biblical words, but they express very well the experience that the biblical prophets seem to have had. The writings of the mystics can help us to interpret the religious experiences of the prophets, and in particular Jesus' exceptionally profound experience of oneness with God. All mystics speak about an experience of union or oneness with God.

Jesus' unique oneness with God has been the subject of centuries of theological debate and of doctrinal and creedal definition.[8] This is not our concern here. Our search is for some clues to the way Jesus might have experienced his oneness with God.

Scholars today would speak of Jesus' experience of union with God as his *abba* experience, his experience of God as his loving Father.[9] Other mystics describe their experience in terms of marriage and sexual union or giving birth to the Son of God or losing oneself and merging with God or with the Absolute. Jesus experienced it as a father-son or parent-child relationship.

All mystics tell us that the words or images we use to describe union with God are inadequate. Nothing can ever convey the wordless, imageless experience of union with God. Nevertheless, we need to use words or metaphors, inadequate as they may be, to speak about this most profound of human experiences. Jesus did it by speaking to God and about God as his *abba*.

One of the strongest memories Jesus' disciples had of him was that he addressed God with a familiar family word, *abba,* rather than any sacred religious word,[10] and that he taught his disciples to do the same. This was so striking and unconventional that the original Aramaic word used by Jesus was sometimes preserved alongside the Greek in the New Testament, as in "*abba* Father" (Mk 14:36; Gal 4:6: Rom 8:15). As a way of addressing and referring to God, it was unique.[11]

In terms of our attempt to understand Jesus' spirituality, the significance of his use of the term *abba* is not that it is masculine or that it is the word a child might use, but that it expresses *intimacy*. God is being spoken of as a loving parent who embraces, holds, and protects his or her child. And, like the love of any good parent, it is warm, unconditional, and totally dependable. Some might associate this more with a caring mother than with a father,[12] although warm, caring fathers are not uncommon these days nor were they in the past.

Still more revealing than his use of the word *abba* is Jesus' description of the loving father in the parable of the prodigal son. This father rejoices at the return of his lost child, gives no thought to punishment or retribution, and does not want to hear anything about his son's debauchery and waste of money. The spontaneous reaction of this *abba* is unconditional forgiveness.

Jesus saw himself as the son who learned by imitating his Father. He learned to forgive unconditionally as God does. He learned to be compassionate as his Father was compassionate (Lk 6:36). Because his Father makes the sun shine and the rain fall on the just and the unjust, Jesus learned to love the just and the unjust, including his enemies and those who persecuted him (Mt 5:44-45 par).

If we find it difficult to take Jesus seriously and to live as he lived, then it is because we have not yet experienced God as our *abba*. The experience of God as his *abba* was the source of Jesus' wisdom, his clarity, his confidence, and his radical freedom. *Without this it is impossible to understand why and how he did the things he did.*[13]

## The Mystico-prophetic Tradition

Not so long ago there was a tendency to separate the spiritual from the political, prayer from work for justice, mysticism from prophetic action. Those who experienced a hunger for spirituality seemed to have no thirst for justice. Politics and the struggle for liberation were felt to be thoroughly mundane and unspiritual. On the other hand, those who were fired with a passion for justice and freedom often thought that resorting to prayer and mysticism was escapist individualism.

There were of course many remarkable exceptions—people who saw prayer and justice as two sides of the same coin. I think of Thomas Merton, Dorothy Day, Oscar Romero, Helder Camara, Dorothee Soelle, Mahatma Gandhi, and numerous others of different faith traditions in South Africa and elsewhere. What interests us here is the powerfully simple way in which prophecy and mysticism form an inseparable whole in the life and spirituality of Jesus.

Today we call it the mystico-prophetic tradition.[14] This term is being used more and more frequently in Christian theology and spirituality, not only as an attempt to overcome the antagonisms between the two in the recent past, but also as a way of recognizing that traditionally, at least in the Judeo-Christian tradition, there was no such division or antagonism. Prophets were mystics and mystics were prophets. Any idea that one could be a prophet calling for justice and social change without some experience of union with God was unthinkable. Equally unthinkable was any idea that one could be a perfectly good mystic without becoming critically outspoken about the injustices of one's time. We often forget that mystics from Basil the Great to Catherine of Siena spoke out boldly against the injustices of the rich, of the political powers, and of church leaders in their times.

These were people who took Jesus seriously and, like Jesus himself, they were rooted in a mystico-prophetic spirituality.

## Institutional Authority

I have always felt that there were two histories of the Christian Church: the history of the institution with its popes and power struggles, its schisms, conflicts, and divisions, its heresy hunting and bureaucracy; and the parallel history of the martyrs, saints, and mystics with their devotion to prayer, humility, and self-sacrifice, their freedom and joy, their boldness and their deep love for everyone and everything. The latter we have come to refer to as the mystico-prophetic tradition, and the former I have chosen to call the tradition of institutional authority.

There has always been a certain amount of overlap between the two, but on the whole these two histories or traditions have run parallel to one another with no small measure of tension and conflict. We have seen how the Hebrew prophets were at loggerheads with religious and political authority, but the same can be said of saints and mystics. Even a cursory glance at Robert Ellsberg's *All Saints*, reveals the remarkable consistency with which the saints and mystics found themselves in conflict, or at least in a tense relationship, with the religious establishment of their time.[15]

Mystics, like prophets, are not appointed by any religious authority to fulfill their role as mystics. The authority of saints, mystics, and prophets has always been based upon their holiness or closeness to God—their experience. And institutional authority has always found it difficult to deal with such freedom of the spirit.

Another notable characteristic of the mystical tradition has been the very large number of women who feature prominently in it, women who wrote extensively about their mystical experiences and acted as advisers and counselors to men and women of all kinds. We have only to think of great mystics like Catherine of Siena, Teresa of Avila, Hildegard of Bingen, Julian of Norwich, Mechthild of Magdeburg, and Catherine of Genoa. On the other hand, the institution has remained solidly patriarchal. Those in authority have been, and still are, men.

What we need to notice about Jesus is that in the conflict between the mystico-prophetic tradition and institutional authority within the Judaism of his time, he was par excellence a representative of the mystico-prophetic tradition. He was not a priest or a scribe. He was a layman—and, to cap it all, a peasant. Institutional authority was represented by the scribes and the Pharisees, the chief priests and the elders, the Sadducees and the Sanhedrin.

But it would be wrong to think that Jesus rejected the religious institution of his time out of hand. He respected the institution as such, "Moses' seat" (Mt 23:2), and he can even be said to have loved all who were part of it. But he totally rejected the way it was being used and abused to oppress the people (Mt 23:3-4). This has been the role of the prophet and the mystic in all religions and faith traditions in all times and places ever since there were religious authorities of any kind.

Both the mystico-prophetic tradition and institutional authority can be misused. Institutional authority can be used to dominate and oppress. On the other hand, charlatans can pose as prophets, mystics, and saints.

Jesus was not an anarchist in the sense that he thought one could manage with no authority structure at all. He wanted to turn the whole religious establishment of his time on its head. And it was with this in mind that he began to build the kingdom-family of God as the new Israel with the new structure of twelve apostles.[16] He seems to have wanted a structure that was more like a family, an egalitarian structure in which those who have authority exercise it as a service to others. When the twelve began to argue about who among them was the greatest, he told them not be like rulers who make their authority felt and lord it over others, but to be like servants who want to serve rather than to be served (Mk 10:42-45 parr).[17] A mystico-prophetic spirituality has relevance also for those who find themselves in positions of authority.

## A Mystico-prophetic Spirituality for Everyone

Anyone who wishes to take Jesus seriously would have to be prepared to become a prophet and a mystic. In the history of Israel before Jesus, prophets were rare individuals. Jesus' aim was to open up the spirit of prophecy to everyone. Anyone can and should read the signs of the times, just as anyone can read the sky and foresee tomorrow's weather (up to a point!) (Mt 16:1-4).

Then too we can all become courageous enough to speak out like prophets. This was the experience of the first Christians after Jesus' death. The outpouring of the Spirit at Pentecost and after was an outpouring of the spirit of prophecy. As Peter says in the Book of Acts (2:17) quoting the prophet Joel (2:28): "In the last days...I will pour out my Spirit upon all flesh, and your sons and your daughters shall prophesy, and your young men shall see visions, and your old men shall dream dreams."

We can also become mystics. In fact, as we have seen, prophecy and mysticism go together. Mystical union with God is not an experience reserved for some very special and privileged people. It is true that everybody does not have the same opportunities for exploring such a possibility. But Jesus did not think that he alone could experience an intimacy with God as his *abba*. God was the *abba* and Father of all: "My Father and your Father" (Jn 20:17); "Our Father" (Mt 6:9 parr). We can all experience some measure of intimacy with God, as we shall see.

According to the frequently quoted prediction of the great twentieth-century theologian, Karl Rahner, "the Christian of the future will be a mystic or will not exist at all."[18]

How we get there is another matter.

## CHAPTER 7

# A Spirituality of Healing

Jesus was a healer. According to Marcus Borg, "More healing stories are told about him than about anybody else in the Jewish tradition."[1] John the Baptist was not a healer. When Jesus moved away from the Baptist and the desert, he returned to Galilee to become a healer.[2] Why?

Some Christians are more than a little embarrassed by Jesus' healing activity. We don't really know what to make of the miraculous cures in the gospels. Can we still believe in miracles today?[3] Besides, we would not like to associate Jesus with most of today's faith healers. And yet we cannot ignore the historical fact that Jesus was a healer.

Perhaps the first thing we ought to notice about Jesus' ministry of healing is that it was holistic.

## Holistic Healing

Our modern distinction between physical and psychological or spiritual healing is not known in the Bible—or in the traditions of Africa. Even when symptoms appear clearly on or in the body, both the illness and the healing are to be understood holistically—as Western doctors are beginning to rediscover today.

Thus, Jesus' healing activity went far beyond the miraculous cures we read about in the gospels. His practice of treating people as unconditionally forgiven, as no longer guilty or sinful, had a powerful healing effect upon those who had been told again and again that they were guilty. One can easily imagine how some people would have been moved to tears by this revelation. We see it in the woman who weeps so copiously that she can be said to have "washed" Jesus feet with her tears (Lk 7:38). "Your sins are forgiven," he says to her. "Your faith has *healed* you; go in peace" (Lk 7:48, 50; my translation). It is important to notice that the same Greek word for healing, *sesoken* (which can be translated variously as "healed," "made well," "restored to health," or "saved") is used in the gospels whether the healing is what we would call physical or what we would call spiritual.

The holistic character of Jesus' healing activity can best be seen in the story of the paralytic who is let down through the roof (Mk 2:2-12 parr). Jesus heals him by saying somewhat surprisingly: "Your sins are forgiven," and then "Stand up and go home." The man was obviously suffering from a serious guilt complex that had paralyzed his whole body. Once he was assured by a prophet like Jesus that his sins were forgiven and that he had nothing more to feel guilty about, he could get up and walk.[4]

The healing effect of Jesus' preaching and teaching can hardly be exaggerated. In turning the world right side up he must have brought untold relief to those who felt overburdened and disadvantaged by the system of the time. With parables and sayings Jesus was trying to open the eyes of his contemporaries to *see* the world differently, to *see* it as it really is—right side up—and above all, to *see* God as our loving and forgiving Father, our *abba*.

"Seeing" was Jesus' preferred metaphor for this kind of consciousness or awareness. "The eye is the lamp of the body," Jesus says, "so, if your eye is *healthy*, your whole body will be full of light" (Mt 6:22 par). On the other hand, some people do not see clearly because they have a log in their eyes (Mt 7:3). It is the truth, seeing things as they really are, that will make you free—that will heal you.

The good news of the kingdom or family of God where everyone will be equal and all things will be shared, and the beginnings of this in the communities that were already forming around Jesus and in the joyful dinner parties for which Jesus was famous, must have been received with enormous gratitude and hopefulness—healing centuries of hurt, resentment, insecurity, and anxiety. What peace and comfort this good news must have brought to an anguished people.

What we need to notice though, is that all Jesus' healing activities were based upon a particular kind of spiritual outlook.

## A Spirituality of Healing

The starting point of Jesus' spirituality, the experience of God as *abba*, included the awareness that God was a loving Father *to all human beings*. God loves and forgives all men, women, and children unconditionally. It was with this conviction that Jesus approached the people of his time.

While he was radically critical of his society, Jesus was never judgmental. He did not blame, accuse, or condemn any individual person. Never once do we find him moralizing, scapegoating, or imputing guilt. His attitude to the people of his time who were labeled "sinners" was strikingly different from the attitude of other religious leaders. They judged and condemned prostitutes, tax collectors, those who did not fast or keep the laws about eating and washing, and those who did not keep the Sabbath or the other commandments.

In turning the assumptions of his time upside down, Jesus rejected any legalistic and moralizing form of religion. To this day, there are people who see religion as nothing more than a system of moral laws and principles sanctioned by God. God makes the laws, judges us in terms of them, and in the next life distributes the appropriate rewards and punishments. The same culture of blame can be found among those who are not religious at all. Whenever there is a problem, people tend to look around for someone to blame. They look for a scapegoat.[5]

## The Sick and the Lost

What was needed, as Jesus saw it, was not blame but healing. In his fellow human beings he saw not sin and guilt but woundedness, brokenness, sickness, confusion, and fear. The people whom the scribes and Pharisees called sinners, Jesus saw as the sick who needed a doctor. "Those who are well have no need of a physician, but those who are sick. I have come to call not the righteous but sinners" (Mk 2:17 parr).

The other metaphor Jesus used to describe the neediness of people was that they were *lost*. The man whom we call the "prodigal" son is, in the parable itself, the "lost" son, like the "lost" sheep and the "lost" coin (Lk 15:1-32). The father in the parable does not see his son as sinful, guilty, prodigal, and in need of punishment. As he says to the older son, "This brother of yours was dead and has come to life; he was lost and has been found" (Lk 15:32).

The lostness or brokenness of the people can hardly be exaggerated. The peasants, as we have seen, were caught up in a spiral of violence with ever increasing taxation and debt, less bread and no food security, more disease and mental illness. Together with the beggars, the prostitutes, and the tax collectors, they were made to feel unclean, guilty, punished by God, and vulnerable to attack by evil spirits. They were lost like sheep without a shepherd—the lost sheep of the house of Israel (Mt 10:6; 15:24; see also Lk 19:10).

But it was not only the poor who lived in a state of insecurity and anxiety. The scribes, the Pharisees, and the rich were also lost, although they would have been reluctant to admit it. They were imprisoned in their own egos, in their self-righteousness and hypocrisy. They were responsible for the terrible suffering of so many others, but deep down they themselves were seriously sick.

What emerges powerfully from the evidence in the gospels and elsewhere is that Jesus was moved by compassion for all who were in need, whatever their pain and hurt might be. His passion was to bring healing to all.

### Beyond Guilt and Blame

When the people ask Jesus whether the Galileans "whose blood Pilate had mingled with their sacrifices," were worse sinners or more guilty than other Galileans, he says no, emphatically no (Lk 13:1-3). And when they ask about the possible guilt of those who died when the tower of Siloam fell on them, again Jesus refuses to impute guilt (Lk 13:4-5). In those days it was commonly thought that tragic accidents were sent by God to punish people for their sins—or for the sins of their parents. In the gospel of John, Jesus is asked whether the blind man was born that way because of the sins of his parents (Jn 9:1-2). The answer as always is no. Jesus is consistent in his refusal to point the finger of blame, to impute guilt.

However, this does not mean that Jesus did not condemn injustice, oppression, selfishness, and sin. When speaking to the scribes and Pharisees he condemns, in no uncertain terms, their pride, arrogance, hypocrisy, self-righteousness, and blindness. But he does not point a finger at any individual and make that person the scapegoat who is to be blamed for Israel's problems. He continues to talk to the scribes and the Pharisees and to eat with them and to teach them—in short, he continues to love them *as individuals*.

More surprising perhaps is the fact that Jesus did not blame or condemn individual Romans either. They were without a doubt the enemy. He knew just how cruelly they oppressed the people and could foresee how merciless they would be when they eventually came to destroy the city of Jerusalem. But he practiced what he preached: he loved his enemies. After all, Romans also needed healing and salvation. And so we find him healing the Roman centurion's son. In the end when the Roman soldiers mock him and crucify him, his only response is to pray: "Father, forgive them; for they do not know what they are doing" (Lk 23:34).[6]


## Two Kinds of Judgment

On the one hand Jesus says, "Do not judge, so that you may not be judged" (Mt 7:1) and on the other hand, apropos of the signs of the times, he says, "Judge for yourselves" (Lk 12:57). These are clearly two different kinds of judgment. The first is imputing guilt and the second is an analysis of right and wrong, of the truth and falsehood of a particular situation.

Jesus was radically critical of his world. Today we would call it a critical social analysis. He turned his social world on its head. But this did not make him bitter and resentful. He did not blame, condemn, or hate any particular person, no matter what they might have done. What he did do, though, was challenge them—all of them.

This is powerfully illustrated in the story of the rich young man (Mk 10:17-25 parr). Jesus was uncompromising in his condemnation of a system that made the rich richer and the poor poorer.[7] It enabled the rich to ignore the poor (Lk 16:19-21) and to believe that they could serve both God *and* Mammon (Lk 16:13 par). Such people could not enter the new family of God any more than a camel could pass through the eye of a needle (Mk 10:25 parr).

*But,* when he meets a rich young man who is obviously trying to serve both God and Mammon, we are told that Jesus "loved him" (Mk 10:21). He does not attack him, blame him, accuse him, humiliate him, or condemn him to hell. Jesus is concerned about him as an individual. He challenges him to sell all his possessions and give the proceeds to the poor. But the young man is unable to accept the challenge and goes away sad—and is not condemned for doing so.

We see the same attitude to individual scribes and Pharisees. Jesus happily accepts Simon the Pharisee's invitation to supper (Lk 7:36).[8] To the scribe who declares that the commandment to love God and neighbor is all that matters, Jesus says, "You are not far from the kingdom of God" (Mk 12:34).

Jesus' respect for the dignity of everyone he encountered was boundless. He treated each individual as unique and lovable —whether that person was a blind beggar, an epileptic, or a Roman centurion. He was particularly attentive to the needs of women and children: the widow of Nain who had lost her only son (Lk 7:11-13), the poor widow who put her last coin into the collection box (Mk 12:41-44 par), the woman suffering from hemorrhages (Mt 9:20-23), the women of Jerusalem who, he says, should weep for themselves and their children rather than for him (Lk 23:28), and, anticipating the day when the Roman armies will attack, the focus of his attention is on children (Lk 19·44), pregnant mothers, and those with babies at the breast (Lk 21:23).

For Jesus, each individual person was unique and important. That is why he could speak about leaving the ninety-nine others to search for the one who was lost (Lk 15:3-6).

## Unconditional Forgiveness

That God loved everyone unconditionally and therefore forgave everyone's sins unconditionally was part of Jesus' unshakeable faith. It was not so much that he came with authority to forgive sins.[9] He did not forgive sins himself. Rather, he told people that God forgave sins unconditionally and that therefore their sins were already forgiven.[10] He did not say, "I forgive you." He said, "Your sins are forgiven" (Mt 9:2 parr; Lk 7:48).

But it was not necessary for Jesus to keep saying this to everyone he met. His attitude, his way of treating them, the attention he gave them, and the way he enjoyed meals with them no matter who they were or what they might have done, spoke louder than words. Here we find Jesus imitating the image of God that he presents in the parable of the lost son. The father's unconditional forgiveness does not require any statement like, "My son, I forgive you" or "Your sins are all forgiven." His open-armed welcome, his obvious joy, and the great celebration he offers his son speak louder than words of forgiveness ever could.

Universal and unconditional forgiveness is beautifully portrayed in the story of the woman who is about to be stoned for adultery—by a crowd of men (Jn 8:3-11).[11] Jesus recognizes immediately the hypocrisy of those who blame, accuse, and condemn the woman. Apart from anything else, it takes two to commit adultery. And who is without guilt of some kind anyway? Who will throw the first stone so as to enable others to join in the mob violence, making of the woman a scapegoat for everyone's sin? In the end, when all her accusers have disappeared, Jesus says, "Neither do I condemn you."

This does not mean that Jesus thought that nobody was ever guilty. Of course we are all guilty, we are all to a greater or lesser extent responsible for our actions. But that is not the point. As far as Jesus was concerned, whatever measure of guilt anyone might have is a matter for forgiveness, not condemnation.[12]

## Healing Relationships

Above all else, it was *by loving people* that Jesus brought healing to them. He loved everyone and identified himself fully with everyone. That is why he could say: "Whatever you do to the least of these my brothers and sisters you do to me" (Mt 25: 40, 45; my translation).

In some cases this would have included real closeness and intimacy. Jesus is often depicted as an isolated individual. In fact, all the evidence points to someone who was not remote and distant, who was not living in some kind of splendid isolation. Apart from the oneness he experienced with all the people he met, Jesus had many close friendships.

Close friendships do not militate against a universal love for all human beings, unless the friendships become in some way exclusive. Jesus' friendships were never exclusive. Being closer to some people than to others is a simple human limitation of space and time. It is physically impossible to have a close relationship with everybody all the time. Besides, we always have more in common with some people than with others.

Friendship with Jesus had a powerful healing effect upon those who were close to him, and, as we shall see, their love for him was not without its effect upon him too.

Peter, James, and John were clearly closer to Jesus than were the other apostles. He would take them with him up the mountain to pray (Lk 9:28 par) and when he was in agony in the garden of Gethsemane the friends he wanted to have with him were the same Peter, James, and John (Mk 14:33 parr). With Peter he had an affectionate but stormy relationship. The effect upon the impetuous Peter must have been deeply healing and transformative.

Then there were Jesus' friends in Bethany: Martha, Mary, and Lazarus. Each in their own way was closely related to him. But the most revealing of all Jesus' friendships, and the closest, was that with Mary Magdalene. She has been confused with the prostitute who "washed" Jesus feet with her tears and with Mary of Bethany. The confusion started in the Middle Ages. Today, as in the early church, she stands out as a remarkable woman in her own right. Mary Magdalene has become the subject of much interest, study, and controversy. Feminist theologians in particular have opened our eyes to the patriarchal suppression of the role she played in the life of Jesus and in the early church.[13]

Mary Magdalene had a deep and unshakeable love for Jesus. She was not afraid to stand at the foot of the cross with Mary his mother when almost all the rest of his disciples had run away (Mk 15:40; Mt 27:55-56; Jn 19:25). She followed those who took down Jesus' body from the cross to see where they would put him (Mk 15:47 parr). Then after the Sabbath, early in the morning, she was there at the tomb to embalm his body, ready to face anyone who might want to stop her. It was she who discovered that the tomb was empty (Jn 20:1 parr). According to John the evangelist, she remained at the tomb and with tears in her eyes continued her search for Jesus' body. She was the first of Jesus' disciples to experience him as risen and alive, and it was to be her vocation to go and tell the others (Jn 20:11-18). Hence her claim to fame as the apostle of the apostles.

Whatever one may think about the account of her controversy with Peter in the Gospel of Mary and other stories about her,[14] she was remembered quite clearly as a strong woman with leadership qualities who was a very close friend of Jesus. There is no evidence whatsoever to suggest that they may have been married.

The love that these and other friends showered upon Jesus must have had an effect upon him. Was it healing for him? To say that would imply that Jesus too was wounded and broken. We have no evidence of that. But what is surely true is that Jesus experienced the love others had for him as yet another manifestation of God's overwhelming love. Apart from his more direct mystical experience of being loved, Jesus must have experienced God's love through the mediation of people—and of nature.

Above and before all else, Jesus must have been influenced by the love of his mother, Mary. A mother's love is not only special; it is irreplaceable. Jesus' life was so free of woundedness, brokenness, and egoism, and his oneness with God was so extraordinary, that we can only conclude that as a child he had been loved unconditionally by Mary—and by Joseph. That would have been an initial manifestation of how deeply his *abba* or divine parent loved him.

## The Power of Faith

Looking at the healing that was breaking out all around him, Jesus saw it as a result of faith. He did not say, "I healed you," or even "God healed you," but "Your faith has healed you" (Mk 5:34 parr; 10:52 par; Lk 17:19; see Mt 9:28-29). In other words, there were no magic formulas or magic wands. This kind of healing was a manifestation of the power of faith.[15] But what is this faith that can move mountains (Mt 17:20 parr)?

In the first place, it is clearly faith in God, not only in the existence of God or even the power of God, but, as Jesus saw it, faith in God as the loving and forgiving Father. Faith is a particular kind of consciousness, the consciousness of God, or the divine, as loving and caring toward us. And that is why the faith Jesus speaks of includes *trust*. Jesus was able to do the things he did because he put all his trust in God. And the lives of others were transformed when they learned to trust God.

The problem with most modern-day faith healers is that when someone is not healed in the way that was expected, they resort to blame. They make the person feel that it is his or her fault, that he or she is guilty of not having enough faith to be healed. That then makes the person's state twice as bad as it was before. The faith that Jesus is talking about means trusting that God will do what is best—which may not be what you or I want. True faith includes praying that God's will may be done.

The secret of Jesus' success as a healer was his extraordinarily powerful faith. He trusted God without hesitation or reserve. He could then quite confidently challenge others to trust God too. He encouraged, strengthened, and liberated people to believe that the impossible could happen. An example of this would be the way in which he challenged the lame, the paralyzed, and the crippled by issuing a simple command: "Stand up and walk." Empowered by his confident faith, people found that suddenly they could stand up and walk. In such circumstances it seems that miracles do happen, that people's lives are transformed. Healing becomes a reality.

Can we imitate this dimension of Jesus' life? We all need healing—as individuals and as a species. How then do we become healers to one another?

# III

# **PERSONAL TRANSFORMATION TODAY**

In Part Three we shift our focus from the signs of our times and the spirituality of Jesus in his time to a practical spirituality for today. What are the practical steps we need to take (if we have not already done so) in order to live in our day as Jesus lived in his?

Healing takes time. There are no shortcuts or quick fixes. A cure or a conversion may happen suddenly and dramatically, but the transformation of the whole person or a whole society takes years, many years—no matter how dedicated we are or how hard we work at it. Jesus called for repentance or conversion, but the legacy he left his disciples was a way, a road, a journey. We must turn the corner, but after that we must move along the road.

Before they came to be called Christians in Antioch (Acts 11:26) and even for a while after that, Jesus' followers spoke of themselves, and were referred to by others, as *people of the Way* (Acts 9:2; 19:9, 23; 22:4; 24:14, 22). I have called it Jesus' spirituality, but we must recognize that this spirituality, like most others, is a process of personal and social transformation, a journey.

All spiritualities and especially mystical spiritualities are structured as journeys with steps or stages. These vary from person to person depending on time, place, and social context. Jesus does not seem to have ever spoken about particular steps or stages, but he was very much aware of the growth and development that would be needed. Hence his parables of the mustard seed and the leaven. He himself "grew in stature and wisdom" (Lk 2:52 NIV). And, as we have seen, his return from the desert to Galilee constituted a new stage in his life and spirituality.

Like all other forms of life, our spiritual life *evolves*, interacting creatively with other people, our environment, and historical events and responding to the opportunities that arise or missing them. The inner work of personal transformation is like a creative work of art rather than like the planned step-by-step journey along a mapped-out road. There is no path that is forever fixed, as some spiritual writers seem to imply. It is, rather, what Meister Eckhart calls a "Wayless Way."

In Part Three, following the inspiration of Jesus himself, we propose some of the changes or mutations that we would have to consider along the road to greater maturity, deeper consciousness, and radical freedom. We will not be alone in walking this and other similar paths of personal transformation. The only way ahead is together, hand in hand, helping and healing one another. And yet, the place to start is with ourselves.

## CHAPTER 8

# In Silence and Solitude

The first hurdle to cross is that of *busyness*. So many people today—executives, politicians, priests, housewives, students, and activists—complain about being overextended. We like to think that there is nothing we can do about it, because there is just so much to be done. With the exception of wage laborers who have very little, if any, control over the number of hours they are forced to work, it is simply not true to say that we can do nothing about our busyness.

Busyness, whether it is a matter of making money or trying to change the world or just doing what others do, has become an obsession. We are driven. We feel obliged to work hard. "Time is money," it is said. "Don't waste time." So many retired people will tell you that they are busier now than ever. We want people to think that we are busy even when we are not. If we don't actually work hard and keep busy, we begin to feel guilty.

Why this obsession with work and busyness? Is it because our lives are empty and we need to fill them with busyness? Are we afraid of having nothing to do? Are we just following the crowd and doing what everyone else does? Or do we actually believe that hard work and tireless activism is all that is needed to save the world?

In truth, busyness is the supreme distraction. It distracts us from self-awareness and from awareness of the *real* world. It distracts us from awareness of God. Busyness leaves us stranded in the upside-down world that Jesus tried to turn right side up. Constant busyness is a bit like sleepwalking. No matter how good our intentions or how altruistic our work, relentless busyness can make us like Don Quixote: fighting windmills instead of real dangers and threats.

Waking up, becoming more fully conscious and facing the realities of life, requires a certain measure of silence and solitude, as it did for Jesus.

### Jesus in the Desert

During the years that we call his "public" life, Jesus was a very busy man. Great crowds followed him, pushing and shoving to get closer to him (Mk 5:24, 31), hoping for healing or a word of wisdom. He and his disciples did not even have time to eat, Mark tells us. They would try to get away to a quiet place to rest a while, but the crowds would follow them and, in his usual caring manner, Jesus would give them his attention once again (Mk 6:31-34 parr). And yet, Jesus seems to have experienced *a profound need for silence and solitude.*

As we saw earlier, he returned as often as he could to the desert. "Desert" here does not mean a hot and sandy place with little or no vegetation. The Greek word *herēmon* means a deserted or lonely place, a quiet place. It was to some such place that he withdrew for forty days and forty nights (and maybe much longer) and to which he went very early in the morning to pray (Mk 1:35). To be alone, he and his disciples sometimes went up a mountain (Mk 9:2 parr; Mk 3:13 par; Jn 6:2). According to Luke, when he needed time to think about his choice of twelve apostles, he spent the night on a mountain (Lk 6:12). The mountain was a deserted place.

If we wish to follow Jesus, we need to follow him first and foremost into the desert. There is no way that you and I today can enter into the spirit of Jesus' Way without creating some space in our lives for silence and solitude. Opportunities for doing this will vary from person to person. In a family with babies or young children, one might need to find time late at night or when the children have gone to school or by visiting a church on the way home from work. A quiet room like a study or a bench in the park may be one's desert or lonely place. Those who live alone or in a religious community will have other opportunities. Those who live in a crowded shack in a slum might have to be more inventive.

It would be best if we could organize a time of peace and quiet every day. But if that is not possible we might try a longer time once or twice a week, perhaps over the weekend. A retreat once a year, valuable as that is in itself, is simply not enough. Regular periods of solitude and silence are indispensable.

Jesus' spirituality is largely about how we relate to people —loving our neighbor. Even our relation to God is most often experienced in our attitude to people. We will look at that in greater detail later. But, like Jesus and all the saints and mystics, we must also find a place in our lives for *solitude*.

The modern psychologist Anthony Storr has written a book entitled *Solitude*.[1] His argument is that searching for happiness and fulfillment in relationships only, as most people try to do today, is mistaken. All the world's geniuses and truly wise men and women benefited from lengthy periods of solitude. To reflect, to discover ourselves and to search for God, we need to spend some time alone.

Similarly, in today's world of incessant noise we need *silence*. We need to find a way of sometimes disconnecting from the relentless flow of words, sounds, and images that bombard us day and night. More important still, we need an inner silence that switches off the inner stream of thoughts, images, and feelings. Without this, authentic spirituality and spiritual transformation would not be possible.

## Silent Meditation

Meditation is not a mental activity like thinking about God or Jesus. Meditation, at least in the way the word is understood today, is an exercise in calming the mind and the heart—as well as the body. It is a way of arriving at inner silence.

Our minds and our hearts are restless. Our heads are cluttered with thoughts and feelings: memories, plans, fears, worries, desires, anger, and frustration. We replay in our heads what happened recently: what we said, what was said to us, what we should have said, and what we will say next time. It is all very busy. In fact, even when we manage to have some quiet time, the noisiness and frenetic busyness of our lives rushes into our minds and hearts. There is outer silence but no inner silence.

What is worse is that we seem to have no control over this jumble of thoughts and feelings. In fact, it is our thoughts and feelings that control and drive us. We are like a cork bobbing up and down on a stormy sea. The more we try to remain calm or to get something out of our heads, the more it returns and occupies our attention. Our chaotic thoughts and feelings drive us to do things we don't really want to do and to say things we know very well we should not be saying.

Meditation is a way of bringing some order and peace into this chaos by emptying our minds of all thoughts and feelings. That is not as impossible as it may sound. There is a way of doing it that has been used with much success over the centuries in Christianity and in the religions of the East.

The first Christian hermits in Egypt and Syria went off into the desert, as Jesus had done, in search of God. For them the first step was *hesychia*, or silence of the heart. This they did mostly through the repetition of what was called the Jesus Prayer: *Lord Jesus Christ have mercy on me*. Linked sometimes to the rhythm of one's breathing, the aim of this practice was the calming of the heart and the mind. As a spiritual exercise, *hesychia* has been practiced in Orthodox Christianity to this day. Some Western mystics adopted and adapted it, especially the fourth-century writer John Cassian, who had a powerful influence on Western spirituality.

The Benedictine monk John Main, who died in 1984, popularized a similar form of meditation using a repetitive word or two that he called a *mantra* (a Sanskrit word used in the religions of the East). Many of us have found this powerfully effective in stilling the mind and silencing the heart.

Numerous other Christians have found peace of mind by following the practice that is known as "centering prayer."[2] In this case the repeated phrase is called one's *sacred word*, but the practice is much the same.

In the religions of the East we have the same experience of calming and emptying the mind through the practice of silent meditation focusing on the rhythm of a mantra and/or one's breathing. Yoga involves concentrating on slow rhythmic movements and controlled breathing while the mind is focused on a word, an object, or a sound like *Om*. The principal religious exercise in Buddhism, especially Zen Buddhism is meditation or *zazen* (sitting still) and the focus is on one's breathing. The mystics of Islam, the Sufis, have the practice of repeating words or phrases, sometimes with special breathing exercises.

What they all have in common is the focusing of attention on one thing: a word, a sound, or one's breathing, and it is this focusing or "centering" that helps to empty the mind of all else. "In the meditation of the great religions," writes William Johnston, "one makes progress by going beyond thought, beyond concepts, beyond images, beyond reasoning, thus entering a deeper state of consciousness or enhanced awareness that is characterized by profound silence."[3]

Thomas Merton once said: "Contemplation is essentially a listening in silence."[4] As the prophet Elijah discovered in his cave on the mountain, God is not in the wind or the earthquake or in the fire but in the silence of a gentle breeze (1 Kgs 19:11-13). Or, as Meister Eckhart would have it, "Nothing is more like God than silence."[5]

We do not know how Jesus prayed and meditated when he went off to a desert or place of silence and solitude. What we do know is that his behavior points to an inner life of perfect calm and tranquility. He showed no sign of emotional restlessness or uncontrollable feelings and thoughts. He was at peace with himself—and with God and the world. Anything that would help us, even partially, to find such calm and tranquility would be a valuable contribution toward living as he did.

### Relaxation

The usual recommendation is that we meditate for twenty minutes twice a day. That would be helpful, but it is not necessary. It is not wise to make meditation into yet another obligation that leads to feelings of guilt whenever we cannot manage it. We do what we can. A certain measure of regularity and discipline is needed, but rigidity prevents the exercise from becoming what it should be, enjoyable and relaxing.

The mantra or sacred word we choose does not need to be particularly meaningful. It is simply a focus point that enables us to forget or ignore our chaotic jumble of thoughts and feelings. When we notice that we have drifted off again to our preoccupations and distractions, we quietly move our attention back to the repetition of the mantra.

Silent meditation is supposed to relax the mind and the heart. But this is possible only if we also do something to relax the body. The spiritual exercise of meditating would be largely ineffective if it did not include some way of releasing the tension in our muscles.

Life today is extremely stressful. The rush and the rivalry, the threats and the dangers, the fears and worries are simply endless. They put our bodies on high alert day and night. Stress in itself is not bad for us. When we are faced with danger, our muscles become tense so as to be ready for flight or fight. When the danger passes, our muscles relax again. But if the "stressors" or things that cause high alert are constant and continuous, our muscles remain tensed up and stiff all the time. That is not healthy. Not only does the body begin to deteriorate, but the tension also affects our behavior and our peace of mind.

There are any number of ways of relaxing the body, from massage and workouts to sporting activities. But, for our purposes, all that is needed is to sit in an upright position during meditation and to relax the muscles of one's face and shoulders where most of the tension lies. If you tighten the muscles of your face, especially the jaw, and then release them, letting your mouth drop, you will notice the difference. Similarly, we hunch up our shoulders because of muscle tension. Releasing those muscles allows our shoulders to drop and relax.

There are other ways of relaxing one's body, mind and heart. Some use music. In Africa there is the continuous repetition of a few words in song. Some Catholics make use of the repetitive prayers of the rosary. But there can no longer be any doubt about the power and effectiveness of silent meditation.

We live in a world that looks for results. The scientific and mechanistic worldview we inherit is interested only in the efficiency and practical results of any exercise. What's more, people want quick results, instant solutions. This is all part of what one might call instrumental thinking or utilitarianism. If it is not useful, throw it away.

Meditation does produce results, but not immediately and not of the kind that can be easily measured. Many people today use meditation in the same way as they use other forms of relaxation—in order to go back to work refreshed and energized. But we do not solve the problem of busyness by simply taking time out in order to come back and work as frenetically as ever. Something more is needed. Time spent in silent meditation can teach us the value of slowing down, of wasting time by doing absolutely nothing, not even thinking. Busy people need to learn the art of doing nothing, the art of just being.

### In the Present Moment

One of the results of spending time in silence and solitude, and especially the practice of silent meditation, is that it helps us to live in the present moment, the here and now. When we empty our minds of thoughts and feelings about the past and the future, all that is left is the silence of the present moment.

According to Matthew (6:25-34) and Luke (12:22-31), Jesus taught his disciples not to worry about tomorrow, what they might eat and what they might wear. Instead, they were to set their hearts on the kingdom or family of God, which, as we saw earlier, is a here-and-now reality, even if it is still as small as a mustard seed. Jesus moved the focus of attention from the kingdom as a future event to a reality of the here and now.

What emerges clearly is that Jesus himself lived in the here and now. He must have experienced God as his *abba* in his present moment. Moreover, this must have been why he would rise early in the morning to find a lonely place to pray in solitude and silence.

Most of us live in the past or in the future. We are distracted by what happened yesterday. Our feelings and thoughts dwell upon what happened recently or sometimes upon what happened a long time ago. We can also romanticize the past.

We might want to go back to the good old days when every-thing was safe, secure, and certain. But the past does not exist anymore. It is not real.

Others live in the future, in the kind of world they hope to have one day, the kind of church or business they hope to cre-ate, the kind of person they would like to be. Or we worry, as Jesus says, about what we will wear and what we will eat in the future. These are imaginary worlds. They don't exist yet. What exists is the here and now, the present moment.

It is valuable to know about the past because the past helps us to understand where we are at present. It is valuable to plan for the future because that can help us to decide what to do now. But the only thing that actually exists is the here and now. And that means that the only place we can meet the living God and experience God's presence is in the here and now. This is why all spiritual writers emphasize the importance of living in the present moment.[6]

Personal transformation begins when we follow Jesus into the desert by setting aside time for silence and solitude. This will be our time for silent meditation, but not only that. We also need time to read, to reflect, to pray, and to allow the spirit of Jesus to seep into our bones. We go into the desert to hear what Jesus has to say and to begin to see the world as it really is. It is our time for getting to know ourselves better, for reading the scriptures and the signs of our times, and for listening to the voice of nature. It all takes time.

Living in the present moment does not mean withdrawing into one's *private* present moment. God is present here and now not only in my private life but also in the lives of everyone and in the whole universe. The present moment that we need to become aware of in silence and solitude is the present moment of today's world. We read the signs of our times in order to live in the here and now of our unfolding universe—which is the only place where God can be found.

I do not wish to imply that we can do these things *only* in silence and solitude. Much can and will be learned through interaction with others. But even the insights we gain from our interaction with people and with the earth need to be integrated into our lives during contemplative periods of silence and solitude. This is what Jesus did, and it is what we also must do.

## CHAPTER 9

# Getting to Know Oneself

According to the Gospel of Thomas, Jesus said: "One who knows everything else but does not know him/herself, knows nothing" (67). A powerful statement. The point could hardly have been made more radically and definitively.

All mystics, spiritual writers, therapists, philosophers, and counselors recognize the fundamental importance of self-knowledge. The psychologist Neville Symington, for example, speaks of self-knowledge as "the foundation-stone of mental health."[1] Teresa of Avila claims that "one day of humble self-knowledge is better than a thousand days of prayer," and Meister Eckhart says quite plainly: "No one can know God who does not first know him/herself."[2] Jesus says if you don't know yourself, *you know nothing.*

Jesus was a poet and an artist who communicated with people by painting mental pictures. In this case he exposed the ludicrousness of not knowing oneself by painting a picture of someone offering to take the speck out of a neighbor's eye while ignoring the huge log of wood in his own eye. It is a cartoon, a caricature. It is meant to be thoroughly laughable, like the equally ludicrous picture of a camel trying to get through the eye of a needle. With a log like that in your eye *you can see nothing.*

We quote the text in full:

Why do you see the speck in your neighbor's eye,
but do not notice the log in your own eye?

Or how can you say to your neighbor,
"Friend, let me take out the speck in your eye,"
when you yourself do not see the log in your own eye?
You hypocrite, first take the log out of your own eye,
and then you will see clearly
to take the speck out of your neighbor's eye.
(Lk 6:41-42)

Jesus goes to the heart of the matter. It is easy to see that other people have blind spots, but we are often not honest enough to recognize the blind spot or huge log of wood in our own eyes. Jesus calls this hypocrisy.

## Hypocrisy

There was nothing Jesus disliked more than hypocrisy. He loved people, but he was enraged by any display of hypocrisy, especially in the religious leaders of his time. "You hypocrites!" he exclaims again and again. The challenge was directed not only at the scribes and Pharisees. Jesus' spirituality challenges all of us to look at ourselves and to recognize our own hypocrisy, the log in our own eye.

To be a hypocrite is to pretend to be what we are not, to present a false image of ourselves to the world. It is about the falsehood of our lives, the lies and contradictions we live. It is about our dishonesty and insincerity, our blindness. If I think I am not blind and that there is no log in *my* eye, then I am doubly blind, blind to my own blindness (see Jn 9:39-41).

Jesus cautions us against parading our virtues before the world like those who pray, fast, and give alms publicly in order to be noticed and admired by others (Mt 6:1-18). They are hypocrites. How easily we become whitened sepulchres (Mt 23:27). How easily the words on our lips contradict what is in our hearts (Mk 7:5-6). How much of our behavior is for show, for the sake of our reputation or image? Jesus would be quite blunt and call it hypocrisy.

Those who say they cannot read the signs of the times but know perfectly well how to read the signs of tomorrow's weather in the sky are hypocrites, Jesus says (Lk 12:56). When we spend time analyzing the performance of our shares on the market while we ignore the stark realities of our times, we have become hypocrites. When we try to catch someone out with a clever question while pretending to be really interested in the answer, then, like those who presented Jesus with a trick question about paying taxes, we are hypocrites (Mk 12:15). We are hypocrites too when we criticize others for doing the very things we ourselves do, like those who criticized Jesus for healing on the Sabbath while they themselves would "break" the Sabbath by untying their ox or donkey to take the animals to the water (Lk 13:15).

The issue here is honesty and truth. Hypocrisy is a blatant lie, a contradiction. Jesus was truthful, honest, sincere, and completely transparent. That is why his eye was clear and he could see the lies and falsehood in the world around him. That is why he could turn the world right side up and show us the *true* world. The yeast or leaven that the Pharisees were kneading into the dough was hypocrisy and lies (Lk 12:1). The leaven of the kingdom that Jesus was spreading was truthfulness and honesty (Lk 13: 20-21 par).

Today, when one of the signs of our times is the crisis of individualism and the explosion of egoism, getting to know who we really are is a matter of extreme urgency. The hunger for spirituality can never find fulfillment if it remains individualistic and self-centered. We know so much more today about everything from stars to atoms. We even know a great deal more about the brain and the human psyche. But in most cases we don't know ourselves. We continue to get ourselves out of perspective by imagining that we are separate from the rest of the universe and superior to all other beings. Too often as individuals we remain blind to our own motives, our rationalizations, our hypocrisy, and the reality of our true selves. As a result there is a very important sense in which we can be said to know nothing.

How then can we learn to face the truth about ourselves in all honesty?

## The Ego

The log in your eye is your ego, your selfish self. What blinds you to the truth about yourself and about others is your ego. What blinds you to the truth about your ego is your ego itself. Our egos make hypocrites of us all.

Although each of us has a slightly differently structured ego, there are ways of categorizing general personality types. One way is through the enneagram. The nine ennea-types point to different compulsions and obsessions, different forms of self-centeredness. The enneagram also details the strengths of the different personality types. In recent times many thousands of people have had their eyes opened to their behavior patterns by books and courses on the enneagram.[3]

The beginning of self-knowledge, then, is our growing awareness of our ego and all its works. Without judging or blaming or making excuses for ourselves, we need to begin the practice of observing our behavior in different circumstances, of recognizing our compulsions and obsessions. We must begin to face as truthfully as we can our motives, including our ulterior motives and mixed motives. Sometimes our behavior may reveal itself as irrational. An honest look at ourselves might reveal that almost all of us are at least mildly neurotic. For some of us, our obsessions may turn out to be seriously neurotic. This is where we will need the help of others: a counselor or a therapist.

As we continue this lifelong process of getting to know ourselves we will notice that we have a variety of *images* of ourselves. Some will be the images we project in company or the images others have of us. Some of these images will be true and others false. At times we may know that this or that image is not true. At other times we may believe our own lies and identify ourselves with a totally false image of who we are.

It can be helpful to observe our ego at work here—tempting us to indulge in feelings of pride and superiority or of abasement and inferiority, of self-righteousness or self-pity. These are all false images, all self-centered and hypocritical. They are not our true self.

The ego is a cunning trickster. It tries to hide from us what it is doing. At times the ego is so convinced of its own superiority that it does not feel the need to boast about it publicly. It assumes a stance of false modesty.[4] "Thank God I am not like other people." We then have the ultimate contradiction and hypocrisy: being proud of our humility.

It would be useful to have a sounding board or mirror, someone who can help us to see the log in our eye. Apart from making use of the expertise of a therapist or counselor when necessary and when possible, patient and honest observation by itself over a long period of time and especially during periods of silence and solitude can lead to quite extraordinary revelations about oneself.

## The Guilt Complex

As we discover more of our selfishness and hypocrisy, we might be tempted to feel thoroughly ashamed of ourselves and even to develop a guilt complex. As we uncover the ulterior motives or mixed motives behind some of our most valued relationships, our greatest achievements, and our highest ideals, we might begin to despair of ever becoming truly unselfish and loving.

Many people suffer from a debilitating guilt complex. It is one of the most irrational and contradictory attitudes of the ego. There are those who hate themselves and blame themselves for whatever goes wrong in their lives. A surprising number of women blame themselves for being raped or assaulted. Children who were sexually abused often think it was their fault.

One source of these guilt feelings is the superego. The superego is all the "oughts" in our head. It is the inner voice that says we ought to do this and avoid that. Some people mistake their superego for the voice of conscience or the voice of God. In fact, it is our cultural, social, or religious conditioning acting as an ego above our own ego—a super-ego. Getting to know ourseves will include a growing awareness of our guilt feelings, our social conditioning, and our superego.

There are of course genuine feelings of guilt and an authentic voice of conscience, but these are manifestations of our true self, as we shall see. It is important to remember, at all times, that the ego is not our true self. Our self-centered self is a false image of who we are. It is based upon the illusion that we are separate, independent, and autonomous.


## The Flesh

The apostle Paul was painfully aware of what we today call the ego, except that he called it the flesh (*sarx*). This has led to a great deal of misunderstanding, because the word conjures up images of sexual desire, over-indulgence, and gluttony.[5] But when Paul lists the works of the flesh he includes hostility, conflict, jealousy, anger, rivalries, divisions, factions, envy, conceit, and competitiveness (Gal 5:19-21, 26). These we would describe as the works of the ego. The desires Paul speaks about, such as fornication, impurity, and drunkenness, are also works of the ego, not because they are desires but because they are selfish or self-indulgent desires.

There is nothing wrong with our desires as such—any of our desires. It is the ego's use of desire for selfish purposes that creates a problem. Our desires have been given to us as gifts to enable us to live life to the full. Our desires for sex, for love, for food and drink, for comfort, for peace, and for unity become twisted and distorted by our egotistical self-centeredness. That is what Paul meant by the flesh.

Paul, like most of us, really struggled with this, as we see in Romans 7:14-24. He experienced his ego as another law in him that made him do what he did not want to do. So, he concludes: "If I do what I do not want, it is no longer I [his true self] that do it, but sin [his ego] that dwells within me" (v. 20). What he calls his flesh, or the law of sin in him, we would call ego. This clearly identifies the problem as selfishness rather than desire. For centuries, well-intentioned ascetics crucified their desires because they thought that desire was the flesh that was leading them astray.

Getting to know ourselves today includes learning to recognize our desires for what they are, getting in touch with our feelings, with our emotions, like love, compassion, sadness, depression, fear, anger, resentment, and frustration. We need to become conscious of our changing moods and our possible woundedness from past hurts. As we now know, trying to suppress our feelings, desires, and emotions is not helpful at all. They are not our enemies. What matters is that we do not allow our egos to misuse them for selfish purposes.

Nor is it enough to simply observe our feelings. Sometimes we need to *feel* them. Henri Nouwen, the modern spiritual writer, provides us with a very valuable insight into how to deal with feelings of hurt and woundedness when he says:

> The great challenge is living your wounds through, instead of thinking them through. It is better to cry than to worry, better to feel your wounds deeply than

to understand them, better to let them into your silence than to talk about them.

The choice you face constantly is whether you are taking your wounds to your head or to your heart. In your head you can analyze them.... But no final healing is likely to come from that source. You need to let your wounds go down to your heart. Then you can live through them and discover that they will not destroy you. Your heart is greater than your wounds.[6]

There is no need to be overwhelmed by all of this. What matters is that you begin to discover your *true self*, or what Nouwen would call your heart.

## The True Self

There is no way you can simply conquer your ego or annihilate it, as many ascetics have tried to do. Such efforts only strengthen the ego, because it is your ego that does the fighting or conquering. You cannot destroy it, but you can sideline it and transcend it. You can remove the log from your eye.

Jesus' image for your true self is your clear eye, your eye without a log or any other obstruction. "Take the log out of your own eye, and then you will see clearly" (Lk 6:42). "Your eye is the lamp of your body. If your eye is healthy, your whole body is full of light; but if it is not healthy, your body is full of darkness" (Lk 11:34). Your true self is buried below your ego or false self, below the log of wood.

But how do you remove the log? How do you sideline your ego? How do you become unselfish and egoless?

The first step is to become fully conscious of your ego with all its machinations and duplicity. Your ego's show of confidence masks the reality of its fears, anxieties, worries, and insecurity. The next step is to recognize it as a false image of who you are, an illusion. The final step is to disassociate yourself from it. You stand back from your egocentricity and laugh at it. You objectify it. Once you have made this false image of yourself into an object out there, you can stop identifying with it. In the words used by some spiritual traditions, you become "the witness" who looks at the false image and rejects it. That's not me. I am the witness. The witness is my true self.

We have seen Jesus doing this in the desert. He refused to identify with the false images of himself presented to him by Satan, the cunning trickster representing his ego. The false images take the form of a temptation (Mt 4:1-11 par).

For most of us it takes years of quiet reflection to do this. We drift back again and again to identify with our egos. We are tempted to act or think selfishly, and we fall for it. When we recognize what we have done, we can stop, laugh at ourselves, and return to the position of witness. The process is much the same as the practice of meditation with a mantra. We will be distracted again and again, but each time we gently return to our mantra. Whatever else, we should not feel guilty and blame ourselves for our lapses. They are par for the course.

At the same time, we will begin to notice the signs of our true self. When we start experiencing a strong desire to know the truth about ourselves, no matter how humiliating that truth might turn out to be, this is our true self emerging. When we can laugh at the antics of our ego, it is our true self that is laughing. When we are genuinely moved with feelings of compassion for people in need, that is the real self. When we begin to feel truly grateful for the many gifts that life offers us, we can be quite sure that this does not come from the ego. The ego is totally incapable of gratitude.

Genuine feelings of sorrow and regret as we recognize our own responsibility and guilt for harm done is yet another manifestation of the true self. There will be other signs too, as we shall see in subsequent chapters.

It is important to remember that we cannot get to know ourselves by merely reading about human behavior. We need periods of solitude and silence to deepen our reflections, and while we may need the help of others, in the end it will be during our quiet time that we will take the log out of our eye and recover from our long night of blindness to begin to see the world as it is and as Jesus saw it—right side up.

CHAPTER 10

# With a Grateful Heart

Jesus saw everything in terms of God's love. His appreciation of God as his loving *abba* was not merely an occasional peak experience. Jesus was constantly aware of God moving and acting with love and care in the events of daily life. He experienced God as the one who feeds the birds, clothes the fields, and looks after each human being (Mt 6:26-30 par). In the signs of his times, especially the surprising outbursts of healing and joy, what Jesus saw and experienced was "the finger of God" (Lk 11:20). It was all God's work, the work of a warm, loving, and intimate God.

In practice this meant that Jesus was conscious of everything in life as a gift from God, a blessing. There is no evidence that he just took things for granted. He was deeply grateful for everything. His life must have been filled with prayers of thanksgiving. Only one such prayer has come down to us: "I thank you, Father, for revealing these things not to the learned and the wise but to mere infants" (Lk 10:21 par; my translation).[1] We can extrapolate from this that there were other prayers of thanksgiving for God's many gifts and blessings. Jesus had a grateful heart. His response to God's love was gratitude.

## The Grateful and the Ungrateful

One of the things Jesus really appreciated in the people he met was their gratefulness. This is powerfully depicted in

Luke's story of the woman who "washed" Jesus' feet with her tears (Lk 7:36-50).[2] She had come to anoint his feet with fragrant ointment as a sign of her gratitude for the good news that all her sins had been forgiven. She had presumably been suffering from a terrible sense of guilt. And now she just couldn't stop crying. Her flood of tears began to fall onto Jesus' feet. She tried to wipe her tears up with her hair, and then she could not resist kissing his feet.

Her copious tears, however, were not the tears of sadness or sorrow or even repentance. She wept uncontrollably because she was overcome with joyful gratitude for having been forgiven so much. She knew how deeply she was indebted to God and to Jesus. Simon, on the other hand, the Pharisee in whose house this happened, did not experience the same grateful love because he did not think that he was much in need of forgiveness or that he was particularly indebted to Jesus or to God.

Jesus felt for the woman and fully appreciated her wild gestures of grateful love. Here was someone with a truly grateful heart.

On the other hand, few things made Jesus as angry as a total lack of gratitude and appreciation. This we see in his parable about the unforgiving servant (Mt 18:23-34). The man has been forgiven a colossal debt. In today's currency it would amount to something like ten million dollars. The sum is purposely exaggerated. No servant or slave could possibly have owed his master that amount of money. It's laughable. It's a caricature.

This very fortunate servant then meets a fellow servant who owes him a mere hundred dollars. He flatly refuses to cancel it or roll it over. The man's extraordinary lack of gratitude and appreciation for what he has been given is unbelievable. That is how Jesus saw any human being who did not wish to forgive his or her neighbor. Such a refusal to forgive demonstrates a quite unbelievable ungratefulness to God who has been so good to all of us.

Ungratefulness is the work of the ego. The self-centeredness of the ego prevents it from ever being truly grateful to someone else—even to God. The individualist regards himself or herself as self-made, independent, and not beholden or indebted to anyone. To admit that something might be an undeserved gift is to admit that one might be dependent upon someone else.[3] There are no free gifts. There is no free lunch.

At its worst, the ego sees others as objects to be possessed, used, and exploited. They are all potential threats or competitors. At best, the ego just takes everything for granted.

The person with a grateful heart appreciates the gratuitousness of everything in life. Nothing is taken for granted. My very existence is a gift. I did not create myself. There is no way that I could have earned or deserved or merited my human existence. Everything I *have* is a gift. Other people are sent to me as blessings, even if at times they appear in disguise—a blessing in disguise, we say.

Gratefulness is an alternative attitude to all of life. It enables us to see the world right side up. The grateful heart is a manifestation of one's true self. Nothing sidelines the ego more effectively than a grateful heart.

"To be a saint," says the spiritual writer Ronald Rolheiser, "is to be fuelled by gratitude, nothing more and nothing less."[4] And, according to Gustavo Gutiérrez, the liberation theologian, only one kind of person transforms the world spiritually, someone with a grateful heart.[5]

## Prayers of Thanksgiving

Personal transformation in the spirit of Jesus would have to include the development of a grateful heart. The practice that molds and shapes one's heart toward gratefulness most effectively is the daily practice of praying prayers of thanksgiving. What we need is not the occasional prayer of thanks when something exceptionally good has happened to us. What we need is continuous daily prayers of thanksgiving. As Paul says, "Pray without ceasing; give thanks in all circumstances" (1 Thes 5:17-18). To develop a grateful heart we need to be thanking God day and night, whenever we have a chance and all through our lives.

Moreover, generalized prayers of thanks for everything are not enough. What we need are specific prayers of thanks for specific things: my health, my eyesight, my mind, my experience of life. We can also say prayers of thanksgiving for our friends and relatives, and for all the people and events that have formed us over the years. The list is endless.

We tend to make lists, at least in our minds, of all our complaints, all the things we think we need or want, all the things we don't have. That is why prayers of intercession, asking God for this and that, are so much more popular than prayers of thanksgiving. There is a place for intercession, but on the whole we need to spend more time expressing our gratitude for the countless gifts that have been showered upon us. The writer David Steindl-Rast in his book *Gratefulness, the Heart of Prayer* defines prayer as "grateful living."[6] And Meister Eckhart once said, "If the only prayer I ever say is Thank You . . . that is enough."

But the ego is a cunning trickster. It can use even our prayers of thanksgiving for its own selfish purposes.

### Unselfish Prayers

Prayers of thanksgiving can become selfish. If I thank God for all that *I* have and all that has been given to *me*, without any sense of gratitude for what others have been given, I will end up thoroughly selfish. Thank God I have enough food when others don't. Thank God I am healthy even if others around me are not. Thank God I am safe; I don't know about the others.

Thank God I am honest and compassionate, unlike most other people. That was the prayer of the Pharisee in the parable: "God, I thank you that I am not like other people: thieves, rogues, adulterers, or even like this tax collector" (Lk 18:10-11). That is not the prayer of a truly grateful heart; it is the selfishness and pride of a swollen ego.

A grateful heart will thank God for *everything* that is good—in my life or in the lives of others. It may be difficult to thank God for the good fortune of others who have gifts, achievements, and friends that I do not have, but that is the test of genuine gratefulness. All else is envy and jealousy.

How easily we thank God for what we have, while we envy others who have more or who have some of the things we want. And when someone else is preferred over me, how easy it is to feel jealous instead of thanking God that the other person is now loved and affirmed. A truly grateful heart rejoices over the good fortune of everyone and anyone.

A grateful heart will also read the signs of the times with an eye for what is best for everyone, not just for me. My true self will be grateful for the movement of the spirit that leads postmodern people to search for a new spirituality. My true self will rejoice with all those who benefit from the globalization of the struggle for justice. We can learn to be deeply grateful for the development of compassion and peace anywhere in the world. The truly grateful person will be pleased to discover that others outside of his or her own religious circles can teach him or her something about transcending one's ego. We thank God for that.

And above all we thank God for the discoveries of the new science, our expanding universe and the mystery of it all, that will give future generations such a great advantage over our generation. We can even thank God for the growing awareness of the destructiveness of individualism and the recognition that we are heading for extinction. That awareness, that recognition, could be a blessing in disguise.

## Personal Transformation

Prayers of thanksgiving are deeply transformative. When we practice this kind of prayer daily, for some time and inclusive of others, it changes our attitude to life. It makes us more appreciative of life, of people, and of God. In some cases this can show itself as a change of personality.

When we learn to see everything in life as a free gift, we no long move around with the long face of those who experience life as drudgery, a boring struggle with one problem after another. Instead of being full of complaints, pessimistic, and impossible to please, we become happy, contented, and grateful for what we have. Instead of being cynical and seeing only the negative in people and events, we learn to appreciate the goodness in other people.

A deeply grateful heart can change one's attitude to God too. I no longer just *think* that God is good and *believe* it because I have been told so. I begin to *feel* that God is good and that God loves me—and everyone else.

## In the Midst of Evil

The challenge, though, is to develop and maintain a grateful heart in the midst of intolerable suffering and evil. We don't thank God for what is wrong in the world. When we are surrounded by so much pain and suffering, so many tragedies and so much cruelty, how can we continue with prayers of joyful thanksgiving?

The danger is that in order to maintain our joyful gratitude we play down the suffering and evil in the world or just ignore it. We find it difficult to hold the two together: the glorious giftedness of life and the horrendous suffering that most people experience as daily living. Nor does it help to say that suffering is good for us, or that good can come out of it, or that it is outweighed by the goodness of God's gifts. Worst of all is telling the victims who are oppressed, downtrodden, or abused that they should just accept their fate and thank God for what they do have.

On the other hand, it doesn't help to become bitter and cynical about our suffering world, to despair and to hate all who are cruel and merciless. We cannot allow the evil in the world to destroy in us the spirit of humble gratitude.

If we are going to be honest and sincere, as Jesus was, we must face the full horror of human suffering and allow ourselves to be outraged by the unimaginable cruelty of so many of our fellow human beings. Jesus had no illusions about that and there is no evidence that he ever played it down. He was overcome with compassion for all who were suffering in any way and he abhorred every kind of cruelty and wickedness. But he also had a joyously grateful heart.

Compassion and gratitude are not incompatible. When we allow ourselves to be moved by feelings of sympathy and compassion for others, we are imitating Jesus. In fact we are experiencing something that is divine. Jesus was compassionate because his Father was compassionate, and he taught his followers to be compassionate too—because God is compassionate (Lk 6:36).

Compassion is a gift from God, one of the most powerful of all God's gifts to us. We can therefore thank God for our feelings of compassion without in any way diminishing the reality of the suffering that evoked our feelings of compassion in the first place. We don't thank God for the suffering, but we are pleased to see people waking up gradually to the pain and suffering of others, and to the reality of human cruelty. Human cruelty, of course, is what happens when we humans have no compassion at all, when we lose all feeling for the other, when the ego reigns supreme.

Compassion finds expression in prayers of intercession and in action. The value of prayers of intercession is that they enable us to express our care and concern for others and our recognition of our dependence upon God. But if the compassion is genuine, then prayer will never become a substitute for action. We are compelled to act and to act boldly wherever we can.

Another important factor in the development and maintenance of a grateful heart in the midst of evil is *trust*. Jesus put all his trust in God. He was hopeful and remained hopeful, despite all the pain and suffering, despite all the cruelty and evil, despite all the failures and disappointments. We will be able to develop and maintain a grateful heart not only when we recognize all of life as a gift but also when we learn to put our trust in God. God is at work in our world today and in the future.

Finally there is the problem of my own pain and suffering. I cannot feel joyfully thankful to God when I am angry about my own sufferings and when I am overcome with self-pity. Why does God allow this to happen to me? That is my ego speaking. But then, how does one deal with painful illnesses, tragic accidents, bereavement, and failure? How does one suffer graciously—as Jesus did?

The answer, as we shall see, is to be found in the mystical experience of oneness with God, with ourselves, with others, and with the universe.[7]

CHAPTER 11

# Like a Little Child

Of all the things Jesus turned upside down, none was more surprising and unexpected than his depiction of a little child instead of an adult as the model we should imitate and learn from. The image he put forward as the ideal to strive for was not the image of some great heroic figure, a person of great strength and power, a superstar, or even a wise old man or woman or a Buddha-like contemplative. The image of true greatness that he put before his disciples and lived up to himself was the image of a little child. For Jesus, personal transformation means becoming like a child. Why?

## Humility

When his disciples were arguing about who was the greatest, Jesus put his arm around a little child (Mk 9:36-37 par). According to Jesus, the least or most insignificant persons in the society are the greatest (Lk 9:48). In the society and culture of the time, the child had no standing or status whatsoever. The child was a "nobody." The implication is that Jesus and those who want to follow him are "nobodies," right at the bottom of the social ladder.[1] For Jesus, the child was a model of radical humility (Mt 18:3-4). Those who wish to follow him will have to become as humble as little children.

However, it is important to notice that you cannot become humble by merely deciding to do so. No amount of determination and will power can make you humble. The harder you try, the less you are likely to succeed, because this kind of effort will be the work of your ego. What you can do is become more *aware* of your pride or lack of humility—of your ego.

Humility is a matter of truth, of recognizing the truth about yourself. To imagine that you are superior to other people when you are not, or inferior to others when you are not, would be to have a false image of yourself. Recognizing the truth about yourself entails recognizing the futility of all comparisons in terms of superior and inferior. Competition and rivalry are the work of the ego.

Since the ego is a false image of oneself, the best way to undermine or sideline it is to grow in awareness or consciousness of the truth about oneself without comparing and without competing. In other words, you become as humble as a child by becoming more aware of your true self. The child was Jesus' image of a person's true self.

Fundamental to his choice of the child as a model was Jesus' well-attested love for children. When his disciples wanted to keep the children away from him because the adults were busy with matters of great seriousness and importance, he was indignant and rebuked the disciples (Mk 10:13-14 parr): "Let the children come to me. Don't stop them." Parents were pushing their children forward to have them blessed or just touched by this amazing man of God. But Jesus saw something more in these children, something truly admirable and lovable. In them he saw something of what his kingdom-family was about. "To them belongs the kingdom" (see Mk 10:14-16 par).

Jesus loved children not merely because they are "nobodies" —overlooked and neglected. Jesus loved children because they are not hypocrites. At their stage of life they are still open and sincere—and in a truly remarkable way they are still spontaneously *trusting*.

## Childlike Trust

In the Gospel of Thomas, Jesus is struck by the trust and contentment of infants in their mothers' arms: "Jesus saw infants being suckled. He said to his disciples: These infants taking milk are like those who enter the kingdom" (22a). The reference is to infants, but the attitude of trusting the parent usually continues into childhood before being gradually eroded as the child grows up.

Babies in the womb and after birth have what is called "basic trust."[2] It is pre-conceptual and involuntary—a natural instinct. They experience themselves as one with their environment and have no reason to mistrust anyone or anything. Gradually, as they become more and more independent and as they begin to experience rejection of one kind or another, real or apparent, growing children learn to mistrust, becoming suspicious of others and of their environment. The isolated ego takes over, aggressive, fearful, mistrusting, and wanting to control its environment.

Jesus recognized in children, and even more in infants, the kind of total and unquestioning trust that he had in God, his *abba* Father. In that sense Jesus was exceptionally childlike. That of course is not the usual image people have of him. He has been accorded glorious titles that exalt him far above anything we associate with children. He is depicted as the all powerful, all knowing king of kings and mighty Savior. Describing him as childlike, however, does not mean that he was weak, immature, inexperienced, or naïve. It means that he drew his strength and self-confidence from his childlike trust in God.

We can see this in his amazing fearlessness. He was not afraid of the scribes and Pharisees. He was not afraid of what they would think of him or say about him. He was not afraid of what they or the chief priests or the Sanhedrin or Herod or Pilate might do to him. And at every opportunity he encouraged his disciples and friends by saying: Do not fear; do not worry; trust

God (Mt 6:25-34; 10:19, 26-31 parr). Where other teachers might have had long lists of "do-nots" or prohibitions, Jesus' principal concern seems to have been that people not be paralyzed by fear.

It would be wrong to think that in times of danger Jesus did not experience feelings of fear. We are told that he "sweated" blood in Gethsemane at the prospect of being arrested, tortured, and crucified (Lk 22:44). But he was not paralyzed by his fear; he did not allow it to determine his behavior. He trusted his Father and prayed his famous prayer: "Your will be done" (Mk 14:36 parr). Feelings of fear are natural and indispensable in situations of danger, but what we eventually decide to do in such situations is another matter. Jesus could cope with fear because of his wholehearted trust and confidence in God.

There are still other reasons, I believe, for Jesus' choice of the child as a model. It is not only the humility and trustfulness of our childhood that we need to return to, but also our childhood sense of wonder and playfulness.

## A Sense of Wonder

One of the most remarkable qualities of a healthy child is a sense of wonder. Everything is new and surprising. We have all seen a child spellbound before some natural phenomenon that we take for granted. Most of us have seen the wonder and awe on the face of a child seeing the ocean for the first time. Watching the waves rushing in, bursting onto the beach before returning quietly, the child can hardly believe her eyes. She runs away from the approaching wave and then runs back when the wave recedes. Is the sea just teasing the little one? For a child, who has not been deprived of its childhood in one way or another, life is magical and everything is a miracle.

As we grow up and go to school and learn to cope with the practical demands of the world we live in, we generally lose our sense of wonder. We begin to take everything in life for granted. Instrumental thinking takes over and we become practical and pragmatic. Our sense of wonder is no longer useful. It doesn't enable us to achieve anything. So we suppress it and get on with life. But, according to Einstein, when we do that, we die. He once said: "The most beautiful experience we can have is of the mysterious. The person to whom this emotion is a stranger, who can no longer pause to wonder and stand rapt in awe, is as good as dead." There are people who never lose their sense of wonder (or regain it in later life): artists, poets, mystics, nature lovers, and scientific geniuses like Einstein.

Reading between the lines of the gospels it seems abundantly clear to me that Jesus had a deep sense of wonder. He was enthralled by the beauty of lilies of the field, whose splendor, he felt, far surpassed that of King Solomon in all his regalia (Mt 6:28-29 par). He marveled at the birds of the air that find food without having to sow and reap and store in barns (Mt 6:26 par). He noticed the miracle of wheat that grows quietly and invisibly while the farmer sleeps, "The earth produces of itself, first the stalk, then the head, then the full grain in the head" (Mk 4:28). In all these marvels of nature, Jesus saw the mysterious hand of God. He was a mystic and a poet.[3]

Jesus must surely have noticed that children have an unspoiled sense of wonder. Would that not have been one of the things he loved in children, their fascination with all of life? Would that not have been one of the reasons why he chose the child as a symbol of true spirituality? Would that not have been what he meant by welcoming the kingdom like a little child (Mk 10:15 par), namely, with a sense of awe and amazement?

## Wonder Today

An increasing number of people today are retrieving their suppressed sense of wonder. The movement of the new science from a mechanistic worldview to a new worldview that sees a universe full of mystery evokes a profound sense of wonder and fascination in almost everyone who becomes aware of it.[4] In chapter 4 we saw something of the wonders and marvels scientists are discovering every day.

Wonder, however, is not a way of thinking or knowing. Wonder itself does not provide me with new information or new understanding. I see something or hear something or hear about something, and then I just stand there in awe, stunned and spellbound. Wonder isn't even a special kind of feeling or emotion. It is a profound experience, but, more important still, it is a form of consciousness.[5]

Wonder cannot be switched on and off at will. Nor is it the result of hard work and determined effort. All you can do is *allow* it to happen to you. Faced with mystery of one kind or another, a natural phenomenon or a human phenomenon, you can let go and allow your sense of wonder to take over. What then happens is that you are swept away by your consciousness of mystery.

As we have noted, our sense of wonder is of itself *useless*. It does not contribute directly to our success in life or to our moral growth or to any other goal we may set for ourselves—all the things that have to do with instrumental thinking and planning. Its value lies in the fact that it wells up from our true self and not from our ego or false self. The ego cannot make use of genuine wonder for any of its selfish purposes. In fact, the ego cannot control our sense of wonder at all. It can only suppress it.

All mystics insist that their experience of God is not knowledge or understanding. It goes beyond that. It is a kind of unknowing or darkness. Yet it is a reality, a real form of consciousness. It would seem then that mystical consciousness is closely related to awe and wonder. The mystic stands in awe at the mystery of God's love.

An important part of the inner work of personal transformation would be to allow ourselves to be carried away by wonder, as often as we can. Nature would be a good place to start— from flowering plants to birds weaving a nest. The new science provides plenty of material for enthrallment and wonder. I mention two examples: the instructions contained in our genes woven together into a single DNA strand in each of our human cells would fill a thousand books of six hundred pages each! And we have billions of cells in our bodies. Our brains are more complex than any human technology. There are 100 billion nerve centers in the brain and each of them has up to 150,000 connections! What a marvel we are!

Human technology can also be an object of wonder. A computer is a miracle of human ingenuity. Then there is the marvel of human language. How do we make all the connections and interpret all the nuances and inflections to understand a sentence? And the human face itself is such a marvel of expressiveness! Eventually we can begin to see everything in the universe as a miracle and a mystery.

## Playfulness and Joy

Finally, I would like to draw attention to another quality that we associate with childhood: playfulness, laughter, and fun. Children know how to enjoy themselves by pretending. They pretend to be grown-ups (mother, father, nurse, bride, doctor) or to be driving a car or to be frightened by something. We know how children can double up with laughter and excitement when adults agree to pretend and to play with them. Jesus noticed the play-acting of children in the marketplace as they argued about whether they would play at, and sing the songs of, a wedding or a funeral (Lk 7:32 par).

There is a superficial similarity between playfulness and hypocrisy. Both involve pretending to be what one is not. The difference is that the hypocrite is serious, while the child does it for fun. The hypocrite is living a lie. The child knows the truth, and that is what makes it funny. In fact, the best way to deal with one's hypocritical ego is to learn to laugh at it.

Playfulness, like wonder, is one of the childlike qualities we tend to lose as we grow up and become more serious. While we may sometimes laugh and joke, few of us would associate such humor with spirituality and mysticism. But that is far from the truth. In her classical work on mysticism, Evelyn Underhill has a section on the joy, playfulness, and childlike gaiety of the mystics.[6] Jesus in particular is almost always portrayed as singularly humorless and deadly serious.[7] If nothing else, Jesus' love for children would belie such an image.

The problems of the world today are no laughing matter, we say. But as we learn to put our trust in God, really and truly, and as we learn to participate in God's great work with hopefulness and abandon, we will find that, despite everything, we can laugh again and be as carefree and joyful as little children.

## Beyond Childishness

There is a world of difference between being childlike and being childish. To be childlike is to imitate the characteristics of childhood that are deeply human and of permanent value, the attitudes most of us lose, unfortunately, as we grow up: humility and sincerity, basic trust and freedom from cares, a sense of wonder and joyful playfulness.[8] On the other hand, to be childish is to imitate or perpetuate the child's temporary qualities that are immature and based upon the child's lack of experience. To imitate in one's adult years the innocence and naïveté of children is childish. To trust everyone and anyone who comes around, as a child might do through lack of experience, is naïve and immature. Children have to be taught not to trust just anyone on the street. To play with fire, as a child might do out of ignorance of the dangers, would indicate a serious lack of maturity.

A child's trust in God might also be somewhat naïve and immature. The child might picture God as a kind of Father

Christmas who gives us the presents we ask for, or as an invisible person who manipulates things around us to prevent us from stumbling and falling. This is an immature image of God and an immature form of trust that would be inappropriate and childish in an adult.

Unfortunately, this is what putting all one's hope and trust in God means for far too many adults. They imagine that they can trust God to manipulate events in their favor especially if they ask him "nicely." That is not childlike trust; it is childishness based upon an immature understanding of God. We should not blame people for this, but we must also not allow it to cloud our own understanding of childlike trust, the kind of trust that Jesus had.

Childish trust in God is also sometimes used as an excuse for not doing what we can and ought to do ourselves. I am thinking in particular of people who do not get involved in struggles for justice where they could do so, because they believe that all one needs to do is pray and then "let God take care of it." While this kind of trust should be avoided, it should not lead us to overlook the fundamental importance of childlike trust in God. Here everything depends upon the development of a more mature understanding of God, which we will explore later.

Jesus' choice of the little child as a model provides us with an image of the kind of person we need to become if we are to grasp the full significance of his spirituality. We see this in his famous prayer of thanksgiving: "I thank you Father for revealing these things not to the learned and the wise but to mere infants" (Lk 10:21 par; my translation). In other words, Jesus' message can be properly understood only by those who are childlike. Perhaps that is why some would say that the saint who most resembled Jesus was Francis of Assisi—with his childlike humility, his childlike trust in God, his sense of wonder, and his joyful personality.

## CHAPTER 12

# Letting Go

The challenge Jesus addressed to the rich young man was to *let go* of his possessions (Mk 10:21-22 parr). The man simply could not bring himself to do that. He was too strongly attached to his wealth; he was enslaved to his possessions. What was being asked of him was not destitution or deprivation. "Sell your possessions," Jesus said, "then come follow me." The man would have become part of a sharing community and he would have had the security that comes from trusting his brothers and sisters—and God. But he was not sufficiently *detached* to do it.

What Jesus expected of those who followed him was complete detachment. They had to be willing to drop their nets and leave their boats, their homes, and their families (Mk 1:17-20 parr; 10:28-30 parr)—perhaps not for life, but at least for long periods of time while they went around the villages preaching. Moreover, when they were on the road preaching they were expected to travel lightly: no money, no bag, no provisions, no extra clothes (Mk 6:7-10 parr).[1] Like Jesus himself they would have to let go of all worries about food and clothing (Mt 6:25-34 par).

Nor was it only possessions they would have to let go of. They were expected to be detached from their reputations too: "Rejoice . . . when people hate you, and when they exclude you, revile you, and defame you" (Lk 6:22-23 par). And, most demanding of all, they would have to let go of their attachment to their lives: "Those who want to save their life will lose it" (Mk

8:34-35 parr). No wonder we are told to sit down and consider the cost before we think of following Jesus (Lk 14:25-33).

There can be no personal transformation without detachment. But what does that mean for us today?

## Detachment

Detachment is not a popular word today. It seems to imply aloofness and indifference. When we accuse someone of being detached, we usually mean that person lacks feeling or passion for something or somebody. But that is not what the word means in the many spiritual traditions that make use of it. Detachment, properly understood, means *freedom*, inner freedom. And, although it is not a word Jesus used, detachment expresses very well an important element in his spirituality: the ability to let go. In the Christian tradition this has been spoken of as "purity of heart" or as the process of becoming "poor in spirit."

For Meister Eckhart, detachment is more fundamental than love itself, because without freedom from our attachments we cannot love fully and unconditionally.[2] We are not free to love until we are willing to stop clinging to our possessions of one kind or another. Otherwise, like the rich young man, our love and our commitment will always be impeded.

Our egos chain us down with a multitude of attachments. Our egos cling desperately to things, to people, to times and places, to reputation and image, to professions and ministries, to our ideas and practices, to success and to life itself. These are our chains. We need to take a closer look at them.

## Our Attachments

Money and possessions are among the most obvious of our attachments. Our possessions include luxuries, comforts, and pleasures. Not that there is anything wrong with these things in themselves. It is our desperate clinging to them that enslaves us. Enjoying life is not a problem, nor is pleasure and desire. The problem is our selfish inability to let go of these things when we are challenged by the needs of others.

Unless we are planning to join a sharing community, we do not need to give away our money and sell all our possessions. We need to become detached from them. Of course it is easy to think we are detached and that we would be willing to give up anything if need be. The proof of our inner freedom comes when we respond to the needs of others generously and spontaneously. If for the sake of everyone we were challenged to lower our standard of living, would we have the personal freedom to do that?

We can become attached to any number of other things too, like cleanliness, neatness, and order. Good as these things are in themselves, we can become so obsessed with them that they become more important than the feelings of people who are not clean or neat or orderly. Then these things become our chains. They prevent us from giving ourselves to others in love.

The same is true of our likes and dislikes, our preferences in food and drink. Such preferences are harmless in themselves, but how easily we can become compulsive and unyielding about them. That is not freedom.

We can become attached to *people* too. Much of what passes for love in our upside-down world is in fact possessiveness. We cling to people because we think we need them. "I need you" is supposed to be an expression of love. Some people like to be told: "I cannot live without you." True love is not based upon my needs. True love is not possessive. True love gives other people freedom to breathe and to be themselves. Attachment to others and excessive dependence upon them is not love.

Many of us would be willing to give up anything except our *time*. How easily we cling to *our* time like some kind of precious possession. The truly free person is able to say that whoever comes is the right person and whenever that person comes is the right time.[3] We see Jesus doing this when he wants to have some quiet time with his disciples. The people follow them. Jesus is sufficiently detached to attend to their needs and postpone his quiet time (Mk 6:30-34 parr).

Of course, I may need to divide my time among several people and ensure that I still have some time for myself, but can I do this freely? Can I be detached about it?

One of the strongest of all attachments is to one's *reputation*. I might be willing to give up anything except my good name. Jesus' radical freedom included the freedom to do what was best for people, even at the cost of his good name. He caused a scandal by associating with prostitutes and other sinners. He was accused of being a drunkard and a glutton (Mt 11:19 par). Anyone who is attached to his or her public image will be seriously hampered in what he or she can do or say. What will people think? What will they say? Will I lose my reputation for virtue, for kindliness, for punctuality?

The truly free person will even be detached from his or her *ministry or profession*. We can become so attached to our work that, like the rich young man, we could never give that up no matter who asked us to do so. We are enslaved to it with chains that cannot be broken. It is like our enslavement to success. Of course we try to be successful, but what happens when we fail? Would we have the inner freedom to accept failure—as Jesus did?

## Attachment to Ideas and Practices

Some people have a particularly strong attachment to *their ideas*. One gets the impression that such people have identified themselves so completely with their ideas that they think if they were to change them they would lose their identity and just die. Truly free persons are open-minded. Their only commitment is to the truth, whatever that may turn out to be, wherever it may come from, and no matter how much they may have to change their most treasured thoughts and convictions in order to embrace it. Anything else is slavery.

Even more upsetting for some people is the undermining of their long held *certainties*. The challenge they face may not be that of changing one idea for another but rather that of replacing certainties with uncertainty. As we move into a world where many of the things that we took for granted in the past are now being questioned, and when the greatest of our scientists are telling us that they don't know, we can cope only by being truly detached from our own ideas and certainties.

Obsession with absolute certainty is yet another form of slavery. It is a way of finding security without having to put all our trust in God. It is fundamentally no different from clinging to our possessions for security.

The ideas and certainties from which we need to become detached may include our ideas and certainties about God. The search for God progresses as we recognize again and again the inadequacy of our thinking about God. We have to have the freedom to abandon some, if not all, of our former certainties. This can plunge us into a "dark night." But that may be the only way forward toward true union with God.

These chains and attachments are not only ideas but also *practices*, which can be cultural, religious, or spiritual. All the mystics warn us of attachment to devotions. I might find a particular devotional practice helpful and there may be no need to give it up as long as I do not become attached to it. Am I free to give it up if need be? The same is true of the practice of meditation that we spoke about earlier. It can become a chain around my neck if I do not have the inner freedom to do without it when for whatever reason I am called upon to do so. An example might be the need of my neighbor. If someone needs my help here and now and for a long period of time, I might have to give up meditation for the duration.

Meister Eckhart, who preached ceaselessly about contemplation and mystical prayer, urges us to be detached even from our contemplation. In one of his sermons[4] he turns the story of Martha and Mary on its head by seeing Mary at the feet of Jesus as a symbol of someone who has become so attached to contemplation that she is unable to get up and help out in the kitchen when that happens to be what God wants her to do. Mary may have chosen the better part, but even the better part can become an object of attachment.

## Loss

Letting go of our attachments requires self-discipline. It is never easy, although the relief once we have become detached from something is a great joy. In some ways it is like giving up an addiction. We feel so much better afterwards, or at least when we have recovered from the withdrawal symptoms. We are free.

Sometimes instead of our letting go of attachments voluntarily, they are taken away from us. While we are still clinging to our money and possessions, for example, we can suddenly lose all of it or most of it. People to whom we were possessively attached might die. Our public image or reputation may be ruined by circumstances that are beyond our control. Our ideas might be publicly exposed as false.

This kind of loss is generally experienced as a tragedy, but it could also help us to become more detached. It could bring us to the realization that we can actually live without some of the things we were so attached too. It's the hard way. But, for some of us, it may be the only way. Spiritual writers call this "passive purgation."

## The Willingness to Die

We have emphasized the fact that detachment is not a matter of giving up everything but of being willing to give up anything when called upon to do so. That is true inner freedom. In this sense, Jesus was radically free. He was not hindered in his freedom by any attachments at all, not even an attachment to his own life. He was willing to die if that were to become necessary.

We recall Jesus' paradoxical statement that when we try to save our lives, when we cling to our lives, when we are not willing to give up our lives for others, we are already dead. But as soon as we are willing to die, we become fully alive—and free. Most of us walk around with the threat of death hanging over us. We cope by just trying to forget that one day we shall die. Death is, as Paul says, the last enemy. But if we can learn to embrace death, we can take the sting out of it and then be truly free.

The willingness to die is the ultimate detachment. It incorporates all other forms of detachment, because it is the ultimate letting go of our ego.

As we have seen, attachment is the work of the ego. Because the ego itself is an empty illusion, it seeks security and substance in wealth, titles, professions, being the author of a book or any other claim to fame. When we identify ourselves with our ego, we identify with these images of ourselves. Our attachments become our identity and our true self is overlooked. But when we gain our inner freedom, when we become detached from these images and "identities," we are able to sideline or transcend our self-centeredness. Our ego can be seen for what it is, an empty illusion. What is more, we no longer need to preserve or cling to our lives—we can let go.

## Trusting God

None of this is possible without putting one's trust in God. If it were possible to let go of everything without grounding ourselves in God, we would become like an astronaut who has let go of the spaceship and will now float forever in outer space. However, trusting God and being grounded in God does not mean attachment to God. It is not as if we become detached from everything except God, so that in the end we cling desperately to God because there is nothing else left to cling to.

Trusting God, as Jesus did, docs not mean clinging to God; it means letting go of everything so as to surrender ourselves and our lives to God. There is a difference between attachment and surrender. In the end we must become detached from God too. We must let go of God in order to jump into the embrace of a loving Father whom we can trust implicitly. We don't need *to hold on* tightly, because we will *be held*—like a child in the arms of its parents.

There are people who cling to God. They make God into a crutch that they feel they must lean on because they are so wounded. That is understandable enough, and we should never lose our sympathy for such people. But there is a better way. We can let go. We can surrender. We can give ourselves in wild abandonment. We can trust God. Clinging, even clinging to God, is the work of a frightened ego. Surrender and trust come from the depths of our true self.

We do not know how Jesus felt or what he thought as he hung in agony on the cross, but there is a very ancient Christian tradition that he felt abandoned by God. In Mark and Matthew he is depicted as reciting Psalm 22, which begins: "My God, my God, why have you forsaken me" (Mk 15:34-35; Mt 27:46-47). The text is quoted partly in Hebrew and partly in Aramaic: "Eli, Eli, lema sabachthani?"—which is unusual and in itself a good reason for regarding the tradition as very old. But that does not mean that in the end Jesus did not surrender, as he always did, to the mysterious will of God. Luke indicates this by quoting Jesus' last words as: "Father, into your hands I surrender my spirit" (Lk 23:46; my translation).

Becoming free, radically free, takes time. Liberating ourselves from our attachments one by one is the work of a lifetime. It is based upon a growing experience of oneness with God. In that, Jesus, as always, leads the way.

# IV

# JESUS AND THE EXPERIENCE OF ONENESS

In the following chapters we will explore a particular kind of awareness or consciousness. Our focus will not be on theories or ideas about the oneness of all things, but rather upon the *experience* of oneness that all mystics talk about. And what interests us here is that it was par excellence the experience of Jesus himself. In a quite extraordinary and mysterious manner, Jesus was conscious of being one with God, with himself, with others, and with all of God's creation. The result for him and for us, as we try to move in that direction, is radical freedom—the theme of our final chapter.

I have decided to speak of *oneness* rather than unity, union, reconciliation, harmony, peace, or love. Unity and union would seem to imply that there are two or more things that need to be united or unified. Reconciliation contains the idea of bringing together what has been separated and divided. Harmony and peace can suggest that we remain separate while we accommodate one another in order to avoid disharmony and conflict.

Oneness, on the other hand, would seem to imply that we are already one and always have been, and that it is simply a matter of becoming aware or conscious of that oneness. Love, then, as we shall see, is what arises spontaneously when we become aware of our oneness.

In the next four chapters we will explore the experience of oneness with God, with ourselves, with other human beings, and with the entire universe. For convenience we need to explore each of these "onenesses" separately. In reality they cannot be separated because they are one, and they are experienced simultaneously as one.

In much of the literature, this experience of oneness is spoken of as the unitive way, the highest stage of mysticism.

## CHAPTER 13

# One with God

Some of us talk rather easily, even glibly, about God. Jesus didn't. He spoke of God as someone who was very close—intimately close. God was his *abba* (as God is our *abba* also), and yet at the same time Jesus treated God with awesome reverence and respect. He took God seriously and he challenges us to do the same. Jesus was not given to half measures or mediocrity.

Today many people no longer believe in God. Others who profess faith in God often don't take God seriously. Despite their profession of belief, in practice God plays no role in their lives at all. Neither the professed atheists nor these practical atheists should be blamed for this. The word "God" has been seriously misused and misunderstood. Millions have been tortured, killed, exploited, oppressed, and crushed in the name of God. Wars, conquests, crusades, and inquisitions have been conducted for the greater glory of God. In God's name heretics and witches have been burnt to death and great injustices have been perpetrated. God's name has been seriously tainted.

Many of the images of God that we inherit are, to say the least, hopelessly misleading: God as the punishing judge, God as the supreme male patriarch, God as the great egoist who imposes "his" will upon everyone, God as the all-powerful manipulator who sends us earthquakes, floods, and other disasters—a God who is very far away. No wonder some writers are suggesting that we abandon the word "God" altogether. As a word it seems to them to be irredeemable. Hence we find people who will speak of the Absolute, the Divine, Transcendence, Being, Creative Energy (Thomas Berry), the All-Nourishing Abyss (Brian Swimme), or simply the Spirit (Ken Wilber and of course many others). Some contend that we should not abandon the word "God" because, apart from its misuse, the word does have a very rich history. Besides, it is the word that fired and inspired Jesus and his followers. In other words, there are people who believe that it is redeemable. And I agree.

## Unknowing God

The first serious question we need to face is whether we can know anything at all about God. Mystics speak of God as unknowable. Thomas Aquinas says that we do not know what God is; we only know what God is not. Negative theology like this is an ancient Judeo-Christian tradition stretching back to Moses' experience of a hidden God. God is invisible and it is not possible to make any kind of visible picture or statue of God. Nor is it possible to name God adequately. In the end God is nameless, ineffable.

The early Christian writer known to us as Pseudo-Dionysius spoke of mysticism as an experience of God that takes place without words, names, ideas, or any knowledge at all. This has been taken up by almost all Christian mystics over the years as an apt description of what they experience. It is called "apophatic" mysticism. The process of reaching this kind of mystical experience entails abandoning all our images of God, all that we thought we knew about God. The process is sometimes called "unknowing." This does not mean that all our images of God are false or useless. It means that we have to go beyond them all, transcend them, "unknow" them before we can have any genuine *experience* of God. Why is this?

All Christian theologians, past and present, all mystics and many others as well teach that, whatever else, *God is not an object*. We cannot count God as one of the objects in the world, even the greatest of all objects or things. God is not a thing alongside other things, or a being alongside other beings. God is not even an invisible being or a hidden being. That is why some mystics speak of God as nothing, meaning "no-thing." And that is why God cannot become an object of knowledge.

But if God is not an object of any kind at all, then what is God?

## Mystery

The word that has always been used to speak of God and is being used today more than ever by theologians, mystics, and spiritual writers is the word "mystery."[1] A mystery is by definition unknown and unknowable. It can never become an object of knowledge without ceasing to be a mystery. But that does not mean that what we call a mystery is not real. We know *that* it is, even if we do not know *what* it is. This is precisely what we would want to say about God.

What matters is not how much I know about God or whether I can know anything at all about God. What matters is whether God is real to me or not. A mystery can be more real to me than any of the things or people I think I know well. Experienced as mystery, God can be more real and more present to me than anything I can see, hear, smell, taste, or touch.

In a totally unexpected way, science has brought us back to the reality of mystery. What science has now made us aware of, or at least more aware of than we were before, is that our human knowledge is limited, very limited. As we saw in chapter 4, we can know and understand things and processes in the universe up to a point. What lies beyond that is pure mystery as far as the human mind is concerned. In the future our minds and our brains may develop further and this, together with more experiments and discoveries, may open up new vistas, but in the final analysis the universe will remain a giant mystery to us, and we ourselves will remain a part of that mystery.

God is not *a* mystery—one among many mysteries. God is *the* mystery—not just the holy mystery or divine mystery. That too would make God one among many mysteries, albeit a very special mystery. God is in a sense the mysteriousness of all things. You and I are part of the mystery. "Part" is not a very good way of describing what one wants to say here. To put it negatively, I am *not* outside the mystery of all things looking at it like some kind of observer. I must include myself in the mystery that we call God. As Paul says, "In God we live and move and have our being" (Acts 17:28).

I experience myself as a mystery too. We all do. The more we try to understand who and what we are, the more we face the unknown and unknowable, the mystery of you and me. The true self that we have begun to explore and will explore further in the next chapter is a total mystery. We cannot see it or hear it. We cannot smell, taste, or touch it. We know it by its fruits, it manifestations.

The appropriate response to mystery of any kind is wonder. We saw how children can be rendered spellbound by the wonders and marvels they encounter. Wonder is a form of consciousness that is without words or images or understanding. When we recognize God as mystery, our spontaneous response is wonder and awe.

## Close at Hand

Somewhere at the heart of Jesus' spirituality is the awareness of God as near, very near. His use of the intimate family word *abba* implies that God was unusually close to him. Is that not also why he could speak of God's kingdom or reign as close at hand? One of the most important changes that Jesus introduced into the religious thinking and spirituality of his time was the conviction that God was not far away. God's kingdom does not belong to the past or the future, and God is not high in the sky. The mystery of God is "in your midst." Jesus recognized God's presence in the here and now—in his present moment.

The nearness of God to everyone, irrespective of who or what they are, is basic to the teaching of the mystics. The Sufis or Muslim mystics say: "God is closer to me than my jugular vein." Echoing the words of Augustine in his famous *Confessions*, Meister Eckhart says, "God is closer to me than I am to myself: my being depends upon God's being near me and present to me. . . . God is near us, but we are far from God. God is in, we are out. God is at home, we are abroad."[2] God is always close to us, not only when we are good or loving or holy. God is close to us even when we don't believe in God or when we ignore God. We can be far from God in the sense that our thoughts are far away and we are not aware of God's presence. But there is no way that God can ever be in reality far away from us, because if God were far away we would cease to exist. Eckhart warns his young listeners about the dangers of thinking about God as far away.[3]

The challenge then is to grow in awareness of God's presence and closeness. In other words, we must become more conscious of the presence of mystery in us and all around us. The mystery is very close to us. In it we live and move and have our being. Our experience of God begins as an experience of wonder and awe in the presence of mystery, here and now, in everything—including ourselves.

## The Oneness

God is not only closer to me than I am to myself, God is *one with me* and with you. There is a mysterious oneness between God and our true selves, and consciousness of this oneness is at the center of every mystical experience. It is spoken of in many different ways: as God dwelling in me, as my being filled with the Spirit of God, as union with God, as a union of wills, or as something comparable to the experience of sexual oneness, a union of bodies. But in the end the mystics find all these descriptions inadequate. Hence we find descriptions like our deification or divinization, our becoming God.[4] Eckhart will go even further and say that the ground of our being is the same as the ground of God's being.[5] Deep down we are one.

Statements like these have led to accusations of heresy. Are they denying the distinction between the creator and the creature, between the uncreated and the created, between God and the world? What matters for our spiritual practice today is that the mystics experienced a oneness with God that was so overwhelming that no words, no matter how exaggerated, could adequately describe the experience.

What then are we to make of Jesus' experience of oneness with God? What his disciples and friends found so extraordinary about Jesus was not just that he called God his *abba,* but that he identified himself with God. There is a way of identifying oneself with God that is an ego trip of the worst kind. But that is because one begins with an image of God as an egotistical dictator who dominates the world. Jesus identified himself with a humble, compassionate, loving, and serving God, and he was bold enough and confident enough to speak and act as that kind of divinity—without qualification.

Jesus' disciples and friends had never witnessed anything like it before. For years afterwards they struggled to find words to describe their experience of a human person who seemed to identify himself with God. Successive generations have continued with this through centuries of theological debate. Our concern in this book, however, is to find a way of imitating Jesus, not explaining him. Our need is to develop a deeper awareness of *our* oneness with God.

### We Are Loved

Jesus' basic conviction was not only that God is close to us, but also that God loves us. As we have seen, God's unconditional love was the foundation of Jesus' spirituality. But if God is the all-encompassing mystery, how are we to make sense of this love? What would it mean to say that we are loved by the awe-inspiring mystery that is intimately close to us? Can I be loved by a mystery or by *the* mystery?

I can begin by recognizing that the mystery in which I live and move and have my being is not hostile to me and cannot be. I am part of the mystery. The mystery gave birth to me. The mystery must then be more concerned about me than I am about myself. If the mystery of God is closer to me than I am to myself and if we are in some profound sense one, then I have nothing to fear. I will be cared for at all times and in all circumstances. Nothing can really harm me and whatever happens will be for the best. I am loved beyond measure because I am one with the whole mystery of life.

As I gradually become aware of the closeness of the mystery we call God, so do I become aware of the impossibility of being hated and rejected. If the mystery of it all were to hate and reject me, it would be hating and rejecting itself. Just as I am challenged to love my neighbor as myself, so also can I come to recognize that God loves me as God's own self. We are in some mysterious sense *one self.*

### A Personal God

As we go along it becomes more and more difficult to talk about the mystery of God in anything but personal terms. Love is an experience between persons, subject to subject, an I-Thou experience, as the Jewish philosopher Martin Buber used to say. Jesus' image of God was decidedly personal. God was his *abba* Father. The long Hebrew tradition that Jesus inherited had always treated God as a person. Jesus didn't just follow this practice, he underlined it and deepened it. His God was an infinitely loving and intimate person.

Treating God as a person is not the same as treating God as an object. God is not one objective person alongside other persons. Perhaps it is better to say that the mystery we call God is personal rather than *a* person.[6] But more important still is the fact that a person is a subject, not an object.

Being aware of the presence of mystery in us and around us translates easily into an awareness of the presence of a person. In fact, the experience of presence is usually the experience of a person rather than an object. The mystery is more like a subject or a self than an object or a thing. Not that God is a self alongside other selves. As more and more people are saying today, God is the universal Self.

For many of us the process of unlearning or unknowing our previous images of God might include a stage of atheism or at least a period of grappling with a de-personalized God. But as our search continues, and especially if we are learning from Jesus, we will come to experience God in personal terms. This will of course be very different from the childish images of a personal God some of us grew up with. The real problem with a loving personal God, however, is what we call the problem of evil.

## The Problem of Evil

If God is in any sense a free and all-powerful person, why does God allow so much suffering, so much cruel injustice, and such devastating natural disasters as earthquakes, tsunamis, droughts, floods, and hurricanes? This is what makes it so difficult to believe in a personal God. Nor is this a new problem. Throughout history men and women who believe in a personal God or gods have struggled to make sense of it.

It is important to remember that what we are talking about here is mystery. A mystery is by definition unknowable. We cannot make sense of a mystery or of *the* mystery. It is beyond the limits of our very limited human understanding. When quantum physicists look at the behavior of "particles" in the subatomic world, they face a mysterious reality that contradicts the laws of nature witnessed elsewhere in the universe. This simply indicates that what is going on in the subatomic world is beyond our human understanding.

All that we can say about God and the intolerable suffering and horrific evil that engulf us is that we cannot understand it. It is part of the mystery, part of what we cannot comprehend. When we expect God to act as *we* would if *we* were God, we forget our very, very limited understanding and the unimaginable vastness of the mystery of God. It would be like trying to tell God how to organize the subatomic world more intelligibly. This is what Job came to realize after grappling for some time and in all honesty with the problem of suffering and evil.

As the theologian Gordon Kaufman reminds us, "The knowledge of good and evil belongs to God, not to us." In the Genesis story Adam and Eve want to become like God, knowing good and evil (Gn 3:5). All our ideas of what is really evil and what is best for us and for the universe as a whole "must always be regarded as questionable," Kaufman concludes.[7]

Despite all our limitations though, what we *can* understand is what we humans should be doing about suffering and evil. We can use our science and technology, for example, to predict earthquakes, to build houses that do not collapse, to construct dikes to prevent flooding, to save water, to respect the environment, to reduce the emission of greenhouse gases, to make poverty history, and to dismantle the structures of oppression.

## CHAPTER 14

# One with Ourselves

There are Christians who have been led to believe that you should love your neighbor and hate yourself. But the challenge of Jesus' spirituality is to "love your neighbor *as yourself*," which clearly presupposes that you already love yourself.

While loving yourself may appear to be natural and spontaneous, the fact is that many people do not love themselves. They hate themselves. They hate who they are, what they are, and where they are. How many of us would prefer to be somebody else, doing something else, living somewhere else, perhaps with a body that is different from the one we have? Some are ashamed of who they are or what they are. They put on a mask to hide their true identity because they hate what they really are.

Self-love is not the same as selfishness or self-centeredness. Strange as it may sound, selfishness is a form of self-hatred. Selfishness means preferring oneself to everyone else. But love is not a matter of preferring one person to another. That is prejudice. Selfishness is not love of self; it is more like being over-solicitous about oneself. Just as an over-solicitous mother may appear to be a loving mother while in fact she has no real love for her child, my ego's over-solicitousness about me is not love at all. It is selfish prejudice. My ego loves nobody, not even me.

Genuine love is one and undivided. We love everyone, including ourselves, with the same love. As the famous psychiatrist Erich Fromm once said: "Love is an attitude which is the same towards all objects, including myself."¹ In fact, one of the ways of overcoming my selfishness, of undermining my ego, is by learning to love myself as I am. Before we can come to love other people as they are, we need to learn to love ourselves as we are—unconditionally.

We will not be able to overcome our selfishness until we resolve our inner conflicts and learn to live at peace with ourselves. Most of us are divided against ourselves. We need to become whole.

## At Peace with Oneself

Jesus was at peace with himself. Despite his struggle with temptation in the desert, his struggle with fear in Gethsemane, and his anger over the exploitation of the poor in the temple courtyard, Jesus did not live in a state of inner conflict. He loved himself. He loved who he was and what he was. His profound experience of being loved by his Father meant that he experienced himself as lovable.

We are lovable too. God loves each of us unconditionally. There are no "ifs" and "buts." God does not love you and me *on condition that* we do good or try hard or believe or trust fully or whatever else. We cannot "win" God's love by transforming our lives and becoming more detached. Any idea that we are not yet good enough to be pleasing to God implies that God's love is conditional. God loves every human being as he or she is and for what he or she is—"warts and all" as we say. The mystery we call God is not only closer to us than we are to ourselves, but also loves us more than we love ourselves.

Jesus' whole life was an expression of this unconditional love. We saw how he reached out to all the individuals he met, whether they were rulers or beggars, saints or sinners. Every individual person is lovable, no matter how hypocritical he or she might be. Genuine love is always unconditional.

The challenge is to learn to love *ourselves* unconditionally. That would mean accepting ourselves as we are, no matter what we have ever done in our perhaps shady past. We have to learn to forgive ourselves. That is sometimes more difficult than forgiving others because we feel so ashamed and so disappointed with ourselves, so guilty. How could *I* have done something like that?

Jung talks about integrating our shadow or dark side into our personality. We have to learn to accept our weaknesses, our limitations, and our shame. Acceptance is not the same as resignation. Being resigned to my faults and weaknesses means acknowledging reluctantly that I have them, while remaining disappointed and even angry with myself for having such limitations. On the other hand, *accepting* my shadow side means I embrace it and love it as a part of who I am. Resignation perpetuates the inner conflict. Loving acceptance enables me to begin to live at peace with myself. In the final analysis, it is a matter of humility, of embracing the whole truth about myself.

## Loving One's Body

What a considerable number of people have difficulty with is loving their bodies. There are several possible reasons for this. It may be that you have an aging body, a body that is tired, sickly, and wracked with pain, or an ugly body, that is to say, a body that does not conform to the latest standards of beauty and attractiveness. So you come to perceive your body as a burden you have to carry. There are those who were brought up to treat their bodies as a handicap they will be released from when they die.

You can begin to actually hate your body. Because it is not what you want it to be, you can get angry and impatient with it. You can also become afraid of your body because of its seemingly uncontrollable appetites and desires. Of course, what some people fear most of all are their sexual desires. We all have to find a way of happily owning our gender, our sexual orientation, and our desires. For some that can be a long and painful struggle.

Pleasure and pain are an inevitable part of bodily life. Pleasure in itself is a gift from God to be savored and treasured. It becomes a problem only when the ego co-opts it for selfish purposes, when it becomes self-indulgent. Pain is also inevitable and we will want to avoid it, but we should not make the mistake of thinking that happiness means all pleasure and no pain. Happiness is the ability to handle my pain, whatever it may turn out to be, and to postpone or give up pleasure whenever necessary.

The body-soul dichotomy or dualism has created havoc in the spiritual lives of generations of Christians. In reality, the body and the soul form one whole person. Separating them is disastrous. My body is not a separate thing that has been attached to me. I am my body.[2] And if I am to love myself, then I must love my body too, or rather I must love everything that I associate with the word "body," from sex to breathing. The challenge is to become one with myself and with everything in me. More accurately, I need to become aware of myself as one whole organic being and not an amalgam of separate parts.

Nor is it just a matter of accepting my body as it is. If my love of myself includes my body, then I need to embrace my body, care for it, and treat it well. That will mean looking after my health, eating properly, getting enough exercise and rest. Many poor people cannot afford nourishing food. Many workers are not given enough time to rest. When they struggle for a life that is more human and healthy, they are not doing something "unspiritual." They are struggling for the right to live the spirituality Jesus offers us. Any idea that spirituality means neglecting the body is profoundly mistaken.

The asceticism of the past that punished and suppressed the body was an unfortunate deviation from the spirituality Jesus lived and taught. The body or the "flesh" and all the desires and feelings associated with it were wrongly identified as the enemy of the spirit. As we have seen, desires in themselves are good; it is the selfish misuse of desire that creates problems for us. Most of the mystics recognized this. Some of them started out as ascetics engaging in heroic acts of endurance and mortification. But by and large they grew out of that and learned to love themselves and their bodies. Writers like Meister Eckhart discouraged ascetic practices from the start. He replaced physical asceticism with detachment.[3]

We live in an age of heightened awareness of the beauty and the marvels of the body. We have increased appreciation for the joys of the senses: touch, taste, smell, sound, and sight.[4] Selfish over-indulgence can be a distraction, but then selfishness is a problem in every area of life. Being at peace and at one with ourselves is not possible without learning to love our bodies.

## Loving Our True Self

The true self is a good place to start in the practice of learning to love ourselves. Our true self is patently lovable.

In earlier chapters we looked at some of the manifestations of the true self in our experience. When you find yourself moved by compassion for those who are in need, your true self is manifesting itself. When you recognize a moment of honesty and sincerity as you long to know the truth about yourself or about anything else in life, that is the real you. Being overwhelmed by gratitude for all the gifts and graces in your life is something that wells up from your very being. At those moments when you inexplicably acted with courage and uncharacteristic bravery, that also was an impulse that came from something very deep in you. If you have ever experienced the quiet joy of sidelining your ego by doing something for others without any reward, without being thanked, and without anyone even knowing about it, then you are in touch with your true self. And when you are swept away by wonder and awe, you are allowing your true self to take over.

These and other similar experiences are often identified as manifestations of the Holy Spirit, or as God's grace at work in us. That is true and it is important to recognize that God dwells in us and that God is closer to us than we are to ourselves. But we should not see manifestations of love as having nothing at all to do with us. If we think that, we are identifying ourselves exclusively with our egos. God works in us but God does so through our true selves. In fact, it is precisely this experience that led the mystics to speak of the oneness of the small, particular self with the greater, universal Self, the mystery of me and the mystery of God. And this is what makes you and me infinitely lovable.

On the other hand, we do have selfish egos, and sometimes we identify with our egos and act out of the self-centeredness that so easily takes over our lives. We should not hate ourselves for doing that. We can laugh at ourselves for such silliness, but it is part of the truth about ourselves that we must learn to embrace so that we can gradually identify more with our true self and less with the false images of ourselves that continue to tempt us.

## Embracing Our Uniqueness

Each of us is unique. There has never been, and there never will be, an individual person like me—or like you. We are not superior or inferior to others, neither better nor worse. But we *are* different—and unique. Each of us has a unique role to play in the mysterious unfolding of the universe. What matters is not whether my role is small or large, or how much time it will require, or whether I will play it as a prominent leader or as a starving child. My role and my contribution, whatever they may turn out to be, are unique. Trying to play another role or someone else's role is pure fantasy.

Jesus was obviously a unique individual with a unique role to play in the history of humankind. He was fully aware of that, but he was also aware of the uniqueness of every other individual. He did not see the person before him as just another beggar or just another Roman soldier or just one of the Pharisees or as yet another rich young man. He saw them as unique individuals. That is why he could love each of them regardless of their labels, appearance, or sins. Even his enemies recognized that he was totally impartial and that he paid no attention to a person's rank or status (Mk 12:14 parr). It was the individual that counted.

Jesus learned this from his Father. God's unconditional love embraces each of us as unique individuals. In fact, God can be said to love our uniqueness. One of the things we learn from the study of evolution is that God loves diversity. Evolution is a creative process that moves forward by reaching out toward a greater and greater diversity of species and of individuals within each species. The number of species that have existed, continue to exist, and will evolve in the future is beyond counting. We are part of an immense universe of great diversity and complexity, but we are not lost and forgotten. Each of us is unique and uniquely lovable.

Selfish individualism is a distorted way of understanding one's uniqueness. Individualists understand their uniqueness as setting them apart. They see themselves as separate and independent, as unique because they are the center of the universe. Uniqueness for them means superior or better or more important than others: "I am unique and everyone else is just another competitor or an obstacle in my way." The ego does not appreciate the true value of everyone's uniqueness.

The opposite of individualism, however, is not collectivism. We do not need to destroy our individuality in order to live in unity with others. The development of an individual self over the centuries has been a great gain for the human race.[5] We should not try to go back to a time when we lived and acted together as tribes or nations without personal identities of our own and without being able to make decisions for ourselves. We have discovered ourselves to be unique individuals.

Learning to love ourselves means learning to embrace our irreplaceable uniqueness, which includes our particular strengths and weaknesses, our successes and our failures, our insights and our stupidities, our bodies and our souls.

## Embracing Death

Sooner or later each of us will die. We prefer to forget that. Our self-centered egos do not want to be reminded of death, because death will bring the reign of the ego to an end. After death my true self will continue in the greater Self we call God, but all my false images of myself will go down into the grave with my remains. Nothing cuts my ego down to size more effectively than the thought that one day I will die.

Death is part of life. My death is part of who and what I am. To forget this is to live in some kind of dream world. Each unique individual comes and goes, because part of our uniqueness is the limited time allotted to us. When we embrace our uniqueness, we embrace, among other things, our death.

I can treat my death as my enemy or as my friend. It is my enemy when I see it as cutting short my self-important contribution to the human race and spoiling my plans. Death is my friend when it reminds me that my own unique contribution has its parameters and that life, limited as it is, is a free gift from God. My death reminds me that I am not indispensable. There are many others, human and non-human, in the grand unfolding of this magnificent universe.

Embracing death does not mean a morbid dwelling upon the details of how I will die and what I might have to suffer before I pass away. Embracing death in the here and now means a conscious willingness to die, whatever the circumstances of my death might turn out to be. This is what Jesus did. He was free because he had already embraced his death. He was at peace with himself because, among other things, he had made his peace with death.

For you and me today, embracing death is part of the great adventure of learning to love ourselves as we are: one, undivided, and unique.

## CHAPTER 15

# One with Other Human Beings

Loving God and loving one's neighbor are obviously central to Jesus' spirituality. What is strange, though, is that we refer to this as the great *commandment*. How can someone be commanded to love? Love is an emotion that wells up inside us in certain circumstances. It is not a matter of obedience or duty. We can act politely and respectfully toward another person when we are commanded to do so, but we cannot really love someone by simply deciding to do so or by a concerted effort of will power.

Reading between the lines of the gospels I am inclined to think that Jesus did not speak about loving God and neighbor as a commandment or a law. In the gospel of Luke (10:25-28) it is not Jesus who says that loving God and neighbor is the greatest commandment. It is a lawyer. But somewhere along the line this came to be handed down as Jesus' own teaching (Mk 12:28-34; Mt 22:34-40). It *was* Jesus' teaching, but I do not think he intended it to be regarded as a commandment or a law.

In Jesus' understanding, loving God was a grateful and joyful response to God's unconditional love. It was a spontaneous response to the experience of God as a loving, caring Father. This is proclaimed in no uncertain terms in the First Letter of John: "We love because God first loved us" (1 Jn 4:19). In practice many Christians see it the other way around: that we first make a giant effort to obey the commandment to love God, and when, with God's grace, we succeed, God responds by loving us. For Jesus, however, God's love comes first.

The situation is not quite the same with our neighbor. Our neighbor may have no love for us at all. In fact, while loving those who do love us is natural enough, the real issue has to do with loving our enemies, those who hate us and curse us (Lk 6:32-36 par), or even loving those who are very different from us, those we don't know at all or those we do know but who irritate us no end. How do we come to love them?

We could say, as John does in his letter (1 Jn 4:11), that if God loves all our neighbors unconditionally, then we should love them too. But it still takes an effort of will to do that. How do we learn to love our fellow human beings *spontaneously*—as Jesus did?

The clue to genuinely spontaneous love of neighbor is to be found in the words "as yourself": love your neighbor as yourself. If I could learn to see my neighbor as a self like me, or an extension of my self, a greater self, loving my neighbor would be as natural and spontaneous as loving myself. What is required is a fundamental change of consciousness—how we *see* our fellow human beings.


## Relationships

We begin with those nearby: our family, friends, acquaintances, and colleagues. With them we speak about having a relationship. We have already noticed that Jesus also had a close circle of friends, disciples, and relatives. Apart from his love for all human beings, Jesus had a special relationship with some people.

Our problem is that the ego treats everyone, even those who are close to us, as *objects*. The ego sees them as objects to be used, to be possessed, to be accommodated and cultivated or to be hated and rejected. They may be objects of interest or not; they may be seen as sex objects or even as objects to be pitied, charity cases. But what the self-centered ego never sees them as is *subjects*, that is to say, as persons.

Most of us have learned to move beyond this kind of ego-centricity, but that does not mean that we are not sometimes tempted to treat even those close to us as objects. At other times we can and do experience the other person as a person, as a self like us, as someone who has feelings, fears, problems, and hopes just as we have. We describe this as putting oneself in the other person's shoes. What must it feel like to be where they are? What does the world look like from their perspective? Many of our relationships would be improved if we sometimes paused to remind ourselves that the one we are with now is also a person with his or her own thoughts and fears.

Putting oneself into someone else's shoes is a subject-to-subject or I-Thou experience. When we become conscious of a person as another self, we experience a kind of oneness with them. This is the beginning of what we call intimacy. The reference is not only to sexual intimacy, but more broadly to the kind of closeness that enables us to share ourselves, our feelings, and our uniqueness.

Jesus, as we have seen, treated everyone he met—not only his friends—as a unique individual. This was possible because he saw everyone as a person, a subject. Jesus loved his neighbor as himself, as another self. In fact he *identified* himself with all other human beings.

## Identifying with Others

Matthew's final summing up of Jesus' teaching on love of God and neighbor takes the form of a kind of courtroom drama in which the judge must separate the good people from the bad, the sheep from the goats (Mt 25:31-46). The basic teaching comes from Jesus but the use of the final judgment as a technique for dramatizing the teaching belongs to Matthew. None of the other gospels has a story like this, although they all have the same fundamental teaching about loving God and one's neighbor. Matthew's story sharpens our understanding of Jesus' own spirituality in several ways.

In first place, the criterion of judgment in this story is how those who appear before the judge have treated their fellow human beings. No questions are asked about their attitude to God, their faithfulness to their duties or to Sabbath laws or any other laws. The activities that form the core of the judgment are what we would today call "works of mercy." Did you feed the hungry, give drink to the thirsty, welcome the stranger, clothe the naked, care for the sick, and visit those who were in prison? That is what loving your neighbor means in practice; that is the criterion for judging whether you love your neighbor or not.

The second feature of this judgment story is that love of neighbor is seen to be in practice the same as love of God—whether the person being judged is aware of this or not. So, when you fed the hungry, gave drink to the thirsty, welcomed the stranger, clothed the naked, nursed the sick, or visited the prisoner, you did it to God. And when you refused to help the hungry, the thirsty and the naked, when you did not welcome the stranger or when you ignored the sick and the prisoner, you neglected to do these things to God—whether you were aware of this or not. The identification of God and neighbor could not have been expressed more powerfully and effectively.

The third thing to notice is that the judge identifies with the *victims* who were helped or not helped. In the beginning the judge is described as the "Son of Man." A few verses later he is described as the "king." It is not clear whether the judge is God or Jesus or both. God clearly identifies with every human being, so that whatever we do to any of them we do to God. But this is also what Jesus did. His oneness with all other human beings could not have been expressed better than in the words of the judge: "Whatever you do to the least of my brothers and sisters you do to me." Whatever was done to another human person Jesus experienced as done to himself.

The challenge is loud and clear. To follow Jesus today is to identify so completely with all my human brothers and sisters that I am able to say: "Whatever you do to any of them, you do to me." In other words, my identity is not just my unique individual self. My identity is the greater self of the human race.[1] This is not to be understood as simply a metaphor or simile. We are not being challenged to love your neighbor *as if* our neighbor were ourself. The judge in Matthew's story does not say, "When you did this to the least of my brothers and sisters, it was *as if* you did it to me" but rather, "you did it to me." The identification is objective and real. God *is* one with all human beings, and we *are* one with one another, whether we are aware of it or not.

Becoming aware of this is important, because loving one another arises spontaneously out of the discovery and continued awareness of our oneness with one another.

What is being referred to here is the solidarity of kinship. We normally experience this kind of solidarity in relation to our close relatives. A mother identifies so completely with her child that she can say, "Whatever you do to my child, you do to me." Siblings might feel the same way about one another. Even members of an extended family or clan might experience such strong ties of blood that an insult to one is experienced as an insult to the others too.

The bond of kinship is the origin of the love of neighbor in the Hebrew Scriptures. In Leviticus your neighbor is your kinsman or kinswoman (Lv 19:18). You would be expected to love them as you love your very self. This can be extended to the stranger in your midst, the foreigner who lives with you (Lv 19:34; Dt 10:18-19) but not to any one else and certainly not to your enemies.

Jesus extended the solidarity or bond of kinship to the whole human race: "You have heard that it was said, 'You shall love your neighbor and hate your enemy.' But I say to you, Love your enemies..." (Mt 5:43-44). He saw them all as his brothers and sisters and mothers and uncles and aunts. He identified with them—no matter who they were, what they had done, or how they treated him. He would be able to say even of his enemies: "Whatever you do to any of *them,* you do to me."

## One Flesh

We are all one family. We share the same blood and the same ancestry. We are one species, *homo sapiens,* descendants of the first human couple to whom we refer as Adam and Eve.[2] We are one flesh.[3]

I come from my mother's womb—flesh from flesh. I started out as a sperm cell meeting an ovum. Then as a fetus in my mother's womb I went through various stages of development until the day I came forth from her womb as a baby, still totally dependent upon her for survival. My mother came forth from her mother's womb and her mother from an earlier mother. My father came from his mother's womb and so forth. We are all one flesh.

You could say that I started out when my mother and father came together in an act of sexual intercourse, when my mother and father became "one flesh" as Jesus called it, quoting Genesis (Mk 10:8, Gn 2:23-24). We have all been coming out of one another and uniting again to extend ourselves further. Whether we participate in procreative sex or not, whether we give birth to babies or not, we are all one flesh. You are flesh of my flesh and bone of my bone, and I am flesh of your flesh and bone of your bone (Gn 2: 23). We remain one flesh all our lives, no matter what illusions of independence and separateness we may develop in our minds. In reality we are intertwined, interconnected, and interdependent. None of us could survive without others. We would have no language and no knowledge. We belong together. We are one.

When you can recognize your neighbor as your own flesh and blood, it becomes possible to love him or her spontaneously, no matter who that person is or what he or she may have done. It becomes possible to say with Jesus: "Whatever you do to the least of these my brothers and sisters, my family, you do to me."

No matter how I look at it, my real identity is as a member of the human race. My true self is being human with all other human beings. Everything else is secondary. Jesus was not less human than the rest of us. He was more human in that he was more fully aware of his identity as one with all humans.

## Empathy

The best English word to describe what Jesus experienced would be "empathy." The Oxford English Dictionary defines it as "the ability to identify mentally with a person...and so understand his or her feelings." This is the experience we are led to as we gradually become aware of our solidarity with other human beings. Empathy is broader than compassion. We are moved by compassion for those who suffer. But we empathize with people even when they are not suffering. We suffer with those who are suffering, but we also rejoice with those who are happy, we love with those who love, we cry with those who cry, and we struggle with those who struggle. We share their feelings because, like us, they are persons with feelings.

In this way we feel with all those who suffer: the hungry, the homeless, the unemployed, the victims of abuse and exploitation, the sick and the dying, the prisoners, and the lonely. And while we allow their pain to move us, we also empathize with their heroic patience or their anger toward those who make them suffer.

Empathy with the poor leads us to take what we today call an "option for the poor." This is not a matter of preferring the poor. The expression "preferential option for the poor" is misleading. Compassion and empathy have nothing to do with preferences—our preferences or God's preferences. God does not have preferences. To take an option for the poor is to side with the poor against those who make them poor or, in other words, to side with a just cause. Structurally, the cause of the poor is right and just, no matter what individual poor people may be like in their personal and private lives. And the cause of the rich is unjust, no matter how sincere and unaware they may be as individuals.

Empathy extends to all human beings. Can we bring ourselves to feel with people who are superficial, foolish, or neurotic? With those who are wounded and broken, including those who drink too much or take drugs? What about the mentally handicapped or those whose smell is unbearable? We are all members of the same human family.

Can we also learn to have some sympathy and understanding for those who do wrong: thieves and liars, hypocrites and murderers? It is not a matter of giving our approval to what they have done but a way of recognizing that in other circumstances we ourselves could have been like them. Besides, we have seen how Jesus did not blame or impute guilt but sought to forgive and heal.

One of the most moving stories coming out of South Africa is the story of a black clinical psychologist and researcher for the Truth and Reconciliation Commission who spent days interviewing a notorious white policeman, Eugene de Kock, whom the media had dubbed "Prime Evil." To her own surprise, she discovered him, despite everything, to be another human being, a person with his own feelings and problems. In the end she was able to actually forgive him and to publish her experience in a very moving and beautifully written book.[4]

If we appreciate the oneness of the human race, our empathy will also extend to the really good and heroic people in the world whose selfless love exceeds anything you and I have been able to do. Without any envy we rejoice that there are such people and thank God for them. Each one has his or her own unique role to play.

Until we transcend our egos and discover our oneness as humans, we will continue to compare and compete, to make one another suffer, to fight and kill. Our species will survive only if we begin to recognize that we are all one flesh and one family.

## Sharing

In reading the signs of our times, we saw that despite the Western world's excessive individualism, there is a growing desire for unity and a growing awareness of the need for cooperation and working together. Perhaps the excesses of individualism, especially greed, are leading us to a greater awareness of the need for sharing and togetherness. Jesus' insistence upon sharing is of particular relevance here.[5]

Awareness of our oneness and solidarity leads naturally and spontaneously to a spirit of sharing. Any idea that we may be able to love one another without sharing is a romantic illusion. Once we have begun to experience ourselves as one flesh, sharing becomes as natural as feeding our own children.

As we grow in our experience of togetherness and inseparability, we begin to direct all we do and say toward what we call the *common good*. What that means in practice is that we come to see that what is best for everyone is best for us too. There is no possible conflict between our good and the common good. Sharing follows quite naturally from this. There would be no need to force people to share. The fundamental mistake of the socialist countries of the last century was that they forced whole nations to share when the overwhelming majority of the people did not want to share. That is counterproductive and oppressive. What the spirit of Jesus will lead to is a passionate desire to share because your good is my good and together we want nothing but the common good.

## Sharing Communities

Jesus promoted the spirit of sharing by forming small groups or communities of believers who, like brothers and sisters, shared whatever they had. Jesus himself lived in a sharing community with his disciples. Judas, we are told, had the common purse (Jn 12:6). These would be the seeds of Jesus' family-like kingdom.

In the Book of Acts we have a good description of what these communities tried to do:

> All the believers were one in heart and mind.
> No one claimed that any of [their] possessions were
>     [their] own,
> but they shared everything they had...
> There were no needy persons among them.
> For from time to time those who owned lands or houses
>     sold them,
> brought the money from the sales...
> and it was distributed to anyone as (they) had need.
>     (Acts 4:32-35 NIV) [6]

This kind of sharing was very important in the early Christian communities, the "assemblies of the saints," and Paul even extended it to a form of sharing between one community and another when he instituted the great collection for the poorer community of Jerusalem (1 Cor 16:1-4; 2 Cor 9:11-15).[7] That it proved very difficult to maintain and did not last very long in the church was precisely because Jesus' radical spirituality was gradually diluted. The ideal of sharing has been kept alive in monasteries, convents, and other religious communities.

Today more than ever, as we saw in our reading of the signs of our times, we need to find ways of reviving Jesus' spirit of sharing. It is not always easy to see how and where we might begin to share today, but true empathy with others will compel us to search for the best ways to do so in our circumstances. Our solidarity and love for one another cannot remain an abstract idea or a warm feeling. In practice it will have to become, however gradually, an economic reality.

What Jesus had in mind was something more than mere almsgiving or what we call "charity." Sharing means more than giving to the poor out of our abundance. Any attempt to live Jesus' spirituality of oneness in splendid isolation, with nothing more than generous handouts to the poor, simply does not work. Oneness means not only that I identify with others but that they identify with me too. We need one another. There is no kind of perfect spirituality that I can achieve without the help of anyone else. If there really is no one to help me, no one to share with, then my growth will be stunted. That is why Jesus did not confine himself to private conversions and individualistic spiritual achievements. He gathered people together in family-like communities as seeds of the emerging kingdom. It was in such communities that his followers discovered their oneness and solidarity with one another. They healed one another by learning from one another, loving one another, and sharing with one another.

It will be in families and in small sharing groups of one kind or another, in the churches or outside of them, that we today will come to experience something of what it means to be treated as persons and to treat others as persons, and what spontaneous love might mean. It will be from some such base that we will reach out to all our human brothers and sisters in solidarity and love. Some of us will be more fortunate than others with regard to opportunities for mutual loving and sharing, just as some of us are more fortunate than others with regard to opportunities for silence and solitude. Our opportunities, like our roles in life, are different and decidedly unequal. Nevertheless, we are all one flesh.

## CHAPTER 16

# One with the Universe

Full participation in the spirituality of Jesus would have to include some experience of our oneness with the universe. Jesus' extraordinarily profound union with God manifested itself not only in his identification with all human beings, but also in his oneness with nature. Because he lived in a pre-scientific and pre-industrial age, he did not experience nature as a resource to be exploited or as a machine to be manipulated. Jesus experienced all of nature, including humans, as *God's creation.*

Nor would Jesus ever have imagined that God had created the universe in the beginning and then left it to carry on by itself. For Jesus, God was actively caring and providing for all of creation, every day. God feeds the birds, clothes the fields with flowers, lets the sun shine and the rain pour down on the just and the unjust alike (Mt 6:26-30 par: Mt 5:45 par). The whole universe is alive with divine action and creativity. Jesus' attitude to creation would have been shaped by the many beautiful creation psalms and canticles of the Hebrew Scriptures.[1] They would have been the prayers or hymns of the synagogue he grew up in. We have already noted his childlike sense of wonder at the marvels of nature.

What is of particular importance for us to notice here, though, is that Jesus saw humans as an integral part of God's creation. We are creatures alongside the birds of the air and the lilies of the field. God cares and provides for us too. Every hair on our heads has been counted (Mt 10:30 par). Jesus does not see humans as standing above creation and observing it from outside. We are part of it, a very valuable and important part of it, but still part of it. "Do not be afraid," Jesus says, "you are of more value than many sparrows" (Mt 10:31 par; see also Mt 6:26 par). But you are cared for in the same way as sparrows are cared for.

Jesus' experience of oneness was rooted in his experience of God as his *abba*. But God was also like an *abba* or caring Creator to the birds of the air and the lilies of the field, to everyone and everything. Jesus must therefore have experienced himself as a part of nature and its rhythms. He lived in perfect harmony with nature and with himself—and with God. The scripture scholar John Dominic Crossan makes this insightful observation about Jesus' inner peace: "The serenity and security passed by Jesus to his followers derives not from knowing hidden mysteries from past or present but from watching nature's rhythms of here and now."[2]

### The Experience of the Mystics

The mystical experience of oneness with God seems to have always included an experience of oneness with nature and the universe. The classical example of this was the experience of Francis of Assisi. Nobody taught Francis to love the birds and the flowers, the rocks and the forests, the sun and the moon, and to treat them all as his brothers and sisters. His gentleness and tenderness toward all creatures, including human beings—and especially the poor and the lepers—flowed quite simply and naturally from his experience of oneness with God. He experienced himself as intimately one with all of God's creatures.

The uneducated Dominican brother Martin de Porres (1579–1639) clearly had the same experience. While his learned confreres in Lima, Peru, were engaged in study and preaching and liturgies, he fed the hungry, attended to the sick, and had a friendly relationship with the rats in the house. All these things flowed quite spontaneously from his experience of God.[3]

The twentieth-century Jesuit mystic and paleontologist Teilhard de Chardin (1881–1955) loved matter in all its forms and taught generations of us to do the same. He also taught us to see ourselves as part of an evolving universe.

Many people tell of peak experiences in which they suddenly became aware of themselves as blissfully one with the whole universe.[4]

The experience of oneness with other human beings would be incomplete and ineffective without an experience of oneness with the rest of the universe. We are not and could never be an isolated species. As human beings we are part of nature; we belong to the greater community of all living beings. More than that, the sun is our brother, the moon our sister, and the earth our mother. We belong to the great family of creation.

Identifying with nature and the universe as a whole is not an optional extra. For mystical spirituality it is absolutely essential. There is no way that I can discover my identity, my true self, without going out and making contact with nature in one form or another. Being part of nature is my basic identity. This needs to become something more than mere words. It needs to become an *experience*.

Many millions of people are deprived almost completely of any contact with nature—and that is a very serious deprivation. So many live in concrete jungles and urban smog, with a view of the world that excludes much of the sky and the stars, and, most of the time, blocks out even the sun and the moon. The urban poor are deprived not only of food, clothing, shelter, and dignity, but also of any real contact with nature. The challenge,

among other things, is to find our way back to the place where
we belong and to help others to do the same.

Writing off this return to nature as mere sentimentality and
romanticism is profoundly mistaken.


## The Paradigm Shift

While our experience of oneness with the universe today will
have much in common with the experiences of the past—of Jesus
and the mystics—it will also be profoundly different. As we saw in
our chapter on the new science, there has been a paradigm shift in
our understanding of the universe. In other words, we are not talking about a few changes in our understanding of God's creatures,
but a totally new perspective, a new framework within which to
make sense of any of the things we see, hear, taste, smell, or touch.

The new paradigm is a *continuously evolving universe.* All
things have evolved and continue to evolve from an original
explosion of energy that we call the "Big Bang" that occurred
thirteen to fifteen billion years ago. We have known for a long
time about the development of history, the evolution of social
structures and, especially from Darwin, the evolution of all living things one from another. But, as Swimme and Berry point
out, "in every instance the supposition was that the universe itself was there in some stable form."[5] Now we know that the
universe is not in any way a fixed or stable entity but an ongoing process, "an irreversible sequence of transformations."[6] The
universe is not a place. We do not live *in* the universe; we are
part of the process. This is the new paradigm that has shaken
the foundations of all our previous assumptions.

The new paradigm has dissolved the mechanistic view of
things while making nonsense of our attempts to control and
exploit nature for our petty selfish motives. Today's industrial
world is simply out of touch with reality.

Jesus pre-dates all of this. He knew nothing of the mechanistic worldview and the industrial exploitation of nature. Jesus' universe was full of mystery and alive with God's creative energy. It was no mere machine or empty ticking clock. Nevertheless, the evolutionary dimension that has been revealed to us in the new paradigm was unknown to Jesus. In other words, he did not know that God's creative, everyday activity is evolutionary.

That did not prevent Jesus from enjoying a fullness of unity with all creation. But what it does for *us* is provide an unprecedented opportunity for deepening our experience of oneness with the universe and through that our oneness with God. It also provides us with an opportunity to deepen our appreciation of the glory of God manifesting itself in the grandeur and the immensity of this mysteriously unfolding universe.

I say advisedly that it provides us with an *opportunity* to do this. Science, no matter how advanced, is not the same as religious or mystical experience. Nor can science be used to "prove" the truth of mystical experience, as we said earlier. Science simply extends what we can see, hear, taste, smell, and touch, thereby extending the opportunity for much greater wonder, awe, and understanding.

Nevertheless, it would be impossible to exaggerate the magnitude of this opportunity and its possible consequences for mystical spirituality. A surprising number of the new scientists, beginning with Einstein himself, have been led by their discoveries to some form of mysticism. The philosopher Ken Wilber was so fascinated by this phenomenon of scientists speaking like mystics that he made a study of it. One of his conclusions was that all of them made a clear distinction between their science and their mysticism. They are two different human activities or experiences.[7]

At the same time an increasing number of people who are not professional scientists are also developing a mystical spirituality around the new universe story, and it seems to be something that will grow exponentially in the near future.

To explore this new opportunity further, we would do well to look at the three principles that govern the dynamics of our emerging universe: unity, diversity, and subjectivity.[8]

## Unity

Nothing has demonstrated the oneness of the universe more stunningly than the discovery that all things originated in one and the same unimaginably small "singularity" (as they call it), out of which there burst forth a mighty explosion of energy— the Big Bang. Everything, but everything, has evolved out of that singularity: matter and spirit, atoms and stars, chemicals and life forms, you and me. It was Teilhard de Chardin who first pointed out that spirit or consciousness must have been present from the beginning because there is no matter without spirit of some kind.[9]

As humans we are one flesh belonging to one human family. As living beings we belong to the closely-knit family of living organisms that have evolved one from another over the last four billion years. So also, as individual entities we can trace our ancestry back to that first burst of energy. We are products of a spectacularly creative process of developing matter and spirit. We are one with the stars and everything else.

The other great manifestation of unity in the new universe story is our interconnectedness and interdependence. Scientists are now convinced that every event in the long history of this immense universe is connected to every other event. There are no isolated or separate events. Nor does any particular event, as we pointed out in chapter 4, have only one cause or even a series of causes. Every event is ultimately dependent, in one way or another, upon every other event in an unimaginably mysterious web of interdependence.

The mystery of our evolving universe is a mystery of mind-boggling unity or oneness.

## Diversity

The second dynamic in the new understanding of the universe is differentiation. The universe unfolds and expands by a process of endless diversification. Atoms, molecules, and cells come together in a bewildering variety of entities and species. There have been, and still are, countless millions of plant, insect, bird, fish, and animal species. The unfolding of the universe is not blind chance. It favors an increase in diversity, ever-greater complexity, and new depths of consciousness. In that sense evolution does have an overall general direction.

Darwin's idea that species evolve by the simple mechanism of natural selection has been superseded by discoveries in microbiology and genetics that point to a far more complex process of cooperation as well as competition in the web of life.[10]

As Thomas Berry says, following the geneticist, Theodosius Dobzhansky, "the universe in its emergence is neither determined nor random, but creative."[11] In other words, the direction of the universe is not the step-by-step slavish implementation of a preconceived blueprint. That is how we humans make things. That is the way of rational intelligence—fixed and determined. That is not God's way.

What the scientific study of evolution enables us to appreciate all the better today is that the Creator is not like a human manufacturer of goods. God is more like an artist. The universe is not the implementation of a predetermined blueprint, but the magnificent ongoing result of artistic creativity. For that reason too, each of us is unique—a unique work of art. We are not mass-produced.

The scientific evidence provides us with an opportunity to experience something of God's mysterious and continuous creativity in all its variety and beauty. We see the glory of God in the grandeur of a creatively evolving universe.

## Subjectivity

The third dynamic of the new universe story is subjectivity. Generally it is the psychologists, philosophers, and theologians who talk about the subject or the self, and therefore about subjectivity. Scientists talk about objects. But their study of the evolving universe has led scientists to the conclusion that what we are dealing with here is not just collections of objects but self-organizing systems. There are systems within systems, each with an organizing principle or a self of one kind or another. It is a universe of subjects and not merely of objects.

We are part of this universe not only as objects among all the other objects that make up the universe. We are subjects who participate in the subjectivity of the universe. We are persons.

This leads us to the mystery of human consciousness. Beatrice Bruteau puts it well:

> We experience our own consciousness *subjectively*, as subjects, from the inside. All the other levels of organization we observed [earlier in the book] from the outside, objectively, seeing them as objects of our cognition. But in the case of our own consciousness, we do something more than and quite different from knowing it as an object for our cognition. We know it by being it.[12]

Our consciousness, and therefore our subjectivity, cannot be explained, because it is a primary datum. It cannot be explained by reference to anything more simple or primary. The mystery deepens at every turn.

## A Seamless Whole

Oneness with God, with oneself, with others, and with the universe forms a seamless whole. Any attempt at union with

God while remaining alienated from other people and from nature would be pure fantasy. Likewise, an experience of closeness to nature that excludes human beings and one's own personal wholeness would be incomplete and ineffective. A genuine experience of oneness with everybody and everything, however, would include oneness with God, even if one is not fully aware of God's presence, because, as we saw in the story of the sheep and the goats, "whatever you do to the least of these you do to me"—whether we are aware of it or not.

What we are talking about here is one seamless experience of moving out of our self-centeredness and isolation into union with all that is. It is a movement from separation to oneness, from selfishness to love, from ego to God. And while much of it may sound abstract, convoluted, and far removed from the problems and concerns of everyday life, it is in practice an experience of beautiful simplicity—the simplicity we see mirrored in Jesus.

The mysterious author of the Fourth Gospel was clearly a mystic who saw that in the final analysis Jesus was the revelation of *oneness*: his oneness with the Father, the Father's oneness with him and with us, our oneness with one another and with him and with the Father (Jn 17:21-23). Paul spoke of this too, albeit in a very different way, recognizing among other things its cosmic dimensions: ". . . through him [Jesus] God was pleased to reconcile to himself all things, whether on earth or in heaven" (Col 1:20). "So that," he says in another place, "God may be all in all" (1 Cor 15:28).

## God and the Universe

We have looked at our oneness with God, with ourselves, with other humans, and with the universe. What remains is the oneness between God and the universe.

Most theologians and spiritual writers speak about God as both transcendent and immanent. God's transcendence refers to the way in which God transcends or goes beyond the universe. God's immanence refers to the way in which God is within the universe. Transcendence, however, is often misunderstood to mean that in some mysterious way God lives in another world, a spiritual and invisible world, *outside* the universe. At the same time, God's immanence is pictured as God being present everywhere *inside* the universe. But outside and inside are spatial metaphors that are not appropriate and even misleading. There is nothing outside the universe because there is no space outside the time-space continuum of the universe. And because there is no outside, it makes little sense to speak of an inside. The result has been misunderstandings about both the transcendence and the immanence of God.

Despite God's immanence in the world, many believers have been led to imagine that God belongs to another world, a heavenly world, and is therefore far removed from everyday life. But, as we have seen, for Jesus God was very near, in our midst. Jesus may have spoken of God as our *heavenly* Father, but that did not mean that God was far away in another world. God is our intimate, loving *abba*.

Like Jesus, the prophets and the mystics did not make the mistake of assigning God to another, heavenly world. Whatever any of them might have thought about heaven, God for them was present and active in the here and now. Their aim was union with God in the here and now of this world, whatever might happen to them after death. "The day of my spiritual awakening," says the beguine mystic, Mechtild of Magdeburg (1210–1280), "was the day I saw and knew I saw all things in God and God in all things."[13]

In fact, many mystics speak so strongly and emphatically about God's oneness with the universe that they are frequently accused of *pantheism*.[14] Pantheism is the belief that God *is* all things. In other words, there is no difference or distinction be-tween God and the universe. Meister Eckhart is still mistakenly thought to have been a pantheist. While there have been and still are numerous people who are pantheists, this is neither what the mystics of the past were saying nor what today's mys-tical writers wish to say.

Because the emphasis today is on God's immanence and God's deep involvement in everything that is happening in the world, most authors try to avoid pantheism by speaking of *pa-nentheism*. This is the word that is used to emphasize that God is *in* all things. Panentheism has the merit of avoiding panthe-ism on the one hand and a God who lives outside our world on the other hand. But I am not sure that it expresses adequately enough the experience of Jesus and of the mystics. To speak of God as *in* all things is to remain with a spatial metaphor that gives the impression that God is some kind of invisible object inside each being or in the gaps between them. The experience of Jesus and the mystics seems to be that God is *one with the universe*.

This has led some writers to speak of a universal incarna-tion.[15] In this model, God is incarnate in the whole universe and the universe is like God's body.[16] God is one with the universe as a person is one with his or her body. Experiencing oneself and others and the rest of the unfolding universe as God's body manifesting and revealing God at every moment is spiritually powerful—an image to be treasured and explored.

A beautiful example of this can be found in the writings of the early medieval mystic, Hildegard of Bingen (1099–1179). She hears God saying: "I am the breeze that nurtures all things green...I am the rain coming from the dew that causes the grasses to laugh with the joy of life."[17]

My concern would be to keep in mind that God is an un-fathomable mystery and should not be thought of as an object of any kind at all. God can therefore be referred to or experi-enced only as a kind of *subject*. In this sense, God is the subject or self of the universe. God is not an object in the universe or the sum total of all the objects that make up the universe. That would be pantheism. God can be thought of only as a subject or rather *the* subject, the universal subject, the universal Self.[18]

We often personify nature and the universe. We speak of Mother Nature. We say that nature heals. The mathematical physicist Brian Swimme speaks of the universe as wanting diversity, complexity, and centration. He sees the universe as creative, caring, nurturing, and never satisfied.[19] That is how Jesus, the prophets, and the mystics would have spoken about God. God is not the diversity, creativity, or energy of the universe. God is the self who diversifies, creates, and energizes. God is not part of creation but the subject that creates. God is the universe as Creator. We can see the creativity in the unfolding universe, but we cannot see the Creator, in much the same way as we can see objects but we cannot see the acting subject in itself.

In this way we can appreciate God as both immanent and transcendent. God is immanently one with the universe, but at the same time, by being the subject, the Self, the Creator of the universe, God transcends all the objects that can be thought of as making up the universe. Words fail us here. God is the transcendent mystery that can never be described or named but, like all subjectivity and consciousness, can only be indicated or pointed to. In awe and wonder we contemplate the mystery of it all.

It may be thought that by this time we have moved far away from the problems and issues of daily life. But this is not so. Our experience of oneness, limited as it may be, is a powerful experience of healing, reconciliation, harmony, love, and peace. More fundamentally still, it is a gloriously *liberating* experience.

## CHAPTER 17

# Radically Free

Radical means reaching down to the roots. The freedom that Jesus experienced reached down to the very roots of his being. It was the freedom he challenged his followers to strive for, and it is the freedom that challenges us today as we hover on the edge of chaos.

Jesus was stupefyingly free.[1] He was able to stand up and contradict the assumptions, customs, and cultural norms of his society. He interpreted the laws, especially the Sabbath laws, freely and was bold enough to disregard all the sacred traditions about what was clean and unclean. Within that society and its religion he had no authority to do any of that. What he did have was the personal freedom to do God's will regardless of what anyone thought or said.

He was free to love without reserve, to love the poorest of the poor as well as the rich young man. The pious would have been scandalized by the love and concern he showed for prostitutes. The poor would have been puzzled by his friendliness toward the hated and exploitative tax collectors. That people called him a drunkard and a glutton did not prevent him from eating and drinking the unclean food and drink of the poor. In fact, he seems to have found the accusation somewhat amusing (Mt 11:16-19).[2]

Jesus' radical freedom made him completely fearless.[3] Throwing the traders and the moneychangers out of the temple courtyard during the height of the festival season when the authorities were on edge about possible riots or rebellions must have taken extraordinary courage. Jesus feared nobody. When the high priest questioned him about the accusations against him, he remained silent (Mk 14:61). Nor does he seem to have been afraid of Pontius Pilate, the ruthless Roman procurator. Jesus was free to die, to give up his life for the kingdom. He was not attached to anything or anybody, not even to his own life or the success of his mission. His freedom knew no limits because his trust in God knew no limits.

## Our Freedom

The immediate result of attempting to live Jesus' spirituality today is freedom. We learn gradually to let go, to free ourselves from our attachments, to throw away our crutches, to ignore our need for success, and to liberate ourselves from worries about our reputation. Fears, worries, obsessions, and compulsive behavior begin to fade into the background as we learn to laugh at our egos. For some, the greatest relief of all is the experience of freedom from guilt. Our wrongdoing will never be held against us. We are forgiven. We are free.

Discovering the truth about ourselves begins the process of personal liberation. Discovering the truth about today's world, an open and honest recognition of what is happening in the human world and in the universe as a whole, can be a liberating experience. The truth will set you free.

The experience of oneness with everyone and everything in the universe that we have been exploring in this section of the book frees us from the tyranny of our isolated egos. We can breathe again. We can trust God and the universe that speaks to us of a loving God. We can relax. All will be well and all manner of things will be well, as Julian of Norwich so encouragingly says. We are free.

The basis of radical freedom is trust. We become free as we gradually learn to appreciate God's love for us, which leads us to surrender ourselves and to put all our trust in God. "Those who hope in the Lord," says the prophet Isaiah, "will soar on wings like eagles" (Is 40:31 NIV). Trust in God enables us to be fearlessly open-minded, free to explore new and unorthodox avenues of thought. We will even have the freedom to sometimes say in all honesty: "I don't know." More important still, we will be able to say: "It doesn't really matter."

The inner freedom we learn from Jesus enables us to love without reserve, accepting ourselves as we are and all other human beings—including our enemies—as they are. The gradual process of detachment removes the obstacles to love, and we soon find that we are free enough to love the whole universe as St. Francis did.

Finally, the freedom we are talking about enables us to do whatever we need to do at any time. We are free to speak out without fear, to stand up and be counted, to laugh and to cry without inhibition, and to be as humble and playful as a child. It also frees us to give up our lives for others—if need be.

## False Freedoms

Postmodernism is a search for freedom. Many people today do not want to be restricted or constrained by doctrines, dogmas, traditions, rituals, or authorities of any kind. They want to be free to think anything at all and to do whatever they like. Insofar as this is a genuine search for freedom it is to be welcomed as a giant step forward in the evolution of human consciousness. But insofar as the freedom postmodern people are seeking is yet another freedom *of the ego,* rather than freedom *from the ego*, it leads to a false and illusionary form of freedom that is no freedom at all. The attempt at breaking the chains of the past is laudable, but this attempt fails if its only result is to bind us with new chains of egotistical self-centeredness. What is wrong here is not the desire for freedom but the mistaken idea that our egos can set us free.

The hunger for spirituality is a hunger for freedom from materialism. The concern here is to make contact with the mystery beyond what we can see, hear, taste, touch, and smell. This hunger for freedom can also become individualistic and selfish, although it has a better chance of discovering the need to be liberated from one's ego. Many of today's spiritualities are doing this. But there remains the possibility of a false sense of spiritual freedom, a self-centered freedom.

Another of the signs of our times, as we have seen, is associated with Western individualism. This too is based upon a deep longing for freedom. But the freedom it pursues is false. It imagines that freedom means self-sufficiency, independence, and separation from the rest of humankind and from nature. We can now see how mistaken that is and how dangerous. It has brought us to the edge of chaos.

Closely related to this is the false freedom we call licentiousness or self-indulgence. It is the selfish pursuit of every pleasure and luxury that money can buy with complete disregard for the needs or feelings of other people. That is not freedom at all.

When the Empire's rulers promise to bring freedom to the world, one wonders what kind of freedom they have in mind. Certainly not the kind of freedom Jesus had in mind. Do they mean the freedom of Western individualism, the freedom of self-indulgence, the freedom of limitless choice, or the freedom to exploit the poor and the needy? The freedom of the rich and the powerful to oppress the weak is the freedom to deprive others of their freedom. That must be about the most cynical of all the false freedoms of the ego.

Another mistaken belief is that all we need is social liberation. Freedom from political, economic, and social oppression is essential. But when these freedoms are pursued without any concern for personal liberation from slavery to one's ego, they become fragile and even counter-productive. Jesus did not believe that all that was needed was a change in the structures of a society or a religious community and that personal freedom would follow automatically from that. He set out to liberate people personally and socially. Unfree individuals can ruin a free society.

## The Fear of Freedom

On the other hand, there are plenty of people who fear freedom. They cannot face the responsibility of having to de-cide for themselves. They feel more secure and safe when oth-ers make decisions for them, because they don't want to risk making mistakes.

Closely related to this is the fear that some have of giving *others* the freedom to decide for themselves. "They cannot be trusted." "They may make mistakes." "They don't know enough to decide for themselves." "We, the learned and the clever, know what is best for them." "They are like ignorant children." This is the attitude, unfortunately, of far too many church lead-ers. It wasn't Jesus' attitude.

It is the fear of freedom that turns some people into funda-mentalists. They want certainty, authority, and absolute truth. Freedom is thought of as extremely dangerous. There are rea-sons for this and we need to examine them carefully and re-spectfully. The human child takes longer than the offspring of other animals to grow up and mature. This is because there is much more to learn. Most of what we need to know to be ma-ture adults comes from culture rather than instinct. We need a long period of education and training before we can stand on our own feet and make decisions for ourselves. During our childhood we need rules and laws. Obedience is essential and discipline might have to be imposed. For a while there may even be some need for reward and punishment.

While it is assumed that we will gradually outgrow all of this, many human beings don't. They remain, to a greater or lesser degree, childish and dependent. Some even get into positions of authority, leadership, and parenthood without ever becoming fully mature adults. All they know and understand is a form of discipline and obedience that is imposed from outside by promises of rewards and threats of punishment. For such people, freedom is terrifying.

While we should not blame anyone for this, we do need to recognize it as immature and childish. Such people can be challenged to grow up but not many will be able to do so—at least not immediately and quickly. In such cases an imposed form of discipline will remain necessary, as it is for children. This is particularly true if they become a danger to society, like rapists and pedophiles. Their freedom must be restricted. One of the problems we face though, is that sometimes we have a leadership that insists on treating fully adult and responsible people as immature children whom they think need to be disciplined.

Jesus challenges us to become spiritually mature. He challenges us to grow up, to move beyond the restrictions of laws and traditional customs, to become radically free. How? By putting all our trust and hope in God. Not many people in his day were ready for that. Many more, it seems to me, are ready for it today.

## Freeing One Another

In apartheid South Africa we used to say: "No one is free until we are all free." The reference was to social and political liberation, but it applies equally well to personal liberation or rather to a holistic ideal that includes social and personal freedom. We cannot become free all alone in splendid isolation. We need one another. No one becomes free without the help and co-operation of others. We learn from one another, from previous generations, from those with much experience and from those with little. We learn from little children and from those who are childlike. Our freedom is much more than a personal achievement. We free one another, just as we heal one another.

Jesus learned from others too: from his parents, from John the Baptist, from the Hebrew prophets of old, and even from the children whom he loved so much. But, more significantly, Jesus worked for the freedom of those who were downtrodden and overburdened, and in his personal encounters with people he liberated them by telling them that God loved them and that their sins were forgiven.

We can also liberate other people. The first obvious way would be by working for the social liberation of all who are oppressed. But we can also stop oppressing individuals in our families, in the workplace, and in our communities. We dominate, sometimes without even noticing it. Perhaps we are possessive. Perhaps we impose ourselves upon others. We don't get anywhere near the inner freedom Jesus was talking about until we begin to free others from the burdens we place on their shoulders or the chains with which we tie them down. We recall Jesus' challenge to the scribes of his time: "You load people with burdens hard to bear, and you yourselves do not lift a finger to ease them" (Lk 11:46). We can liberate others from the burden of guilt by telling them that we forgive them or that God forgives them.

But what some of us need more than anything else is to allow others to contribute to *our* inner freedom. The pursuit of freedom can become selfish and self-centered. The ego can co-opt our striving for freedom and try to make of it a personal achievement that we can boast about. This can lead us to believe that we don't need the help of others. The fact is that we *can* soar, we *can* fly, but not alone.

Radical freedom is the ideal we aim for. But we may never reach it. Some go further than others. Some never even get started. True freedom begins the day I can say that it doesn't matter how far *I* am along the road to freedom. It doesn't matter whether I have more or less opportunity than others to become free. It doesn't matter whether I die before I can make much progress. Radical freedom includes the freedom not to worry about such things, not to compare and compete.

The paradox then is that true freedom includes the freedom to accept my personal lack of inner freedom. We are all in this together. We each have our different and unique roles to play. What matters is not my personal achievements. What matters is what Jesus called *the will of God*.

## Free to Do God's Will

For Jesus, freedom is not an end in itself; it is a means to something greater, namely, doing the will of God. I am not called to be perfectly free, I am called to do God's will, but I can do this effectively only by trying to become as free as possible. To our modern or postmodern ears, that sounds like a contradiction.

Jesus seems to have made extensive use of the notion of God's will, and so did his followers.[4] In fact, Christians throughout the ages have often centered their spirituality on the idea of doing God's will. Jesus set out to do God's will even when he was sorely tempted not to do it, as in the garden of Gethsemane. In the end there was no contradiction between his will and God's will. Is that freedom?

The problem for us today is that talk about obeying God's will *sounds like oppression and domination*. It sounds as if God is imposing "his" will upon everybody and not allowing us to be free and to decide for ourselves. This is partly because of a false image of God as someone with a great big male ego, and partly because God's will or anybody else's will sounds totally arbitrary. My will is my purely arbitrary choice about what ought to be done. To impose that on others would be decidedly oppressive. That is not at all what Jesus had in mind.

To understand what Jesus meant by God's will, we might best translate it as "the common good." The common good is whatever is best for the whole human family or the whole community of living beings or the whole universe in its grand unfolding. We are not isolated individuals. We are parts of a greater whole and it is the whole that determines the very existence of the parts. A part exists for the good of the whole because the identity of the part is precisely to be a part of this whole.

In a world that is dominated by ego and individualism, it is assumed that the common good contradicts my personal good. In other words, what is good for the whole society is generally not good for me, and what is good for me will clash with the needs of others or the common good. This means that I will sometimes have to *sacrifice* my own good for the good of others.

This is simply not true. There is no contradiction. What is best for everyone is also best for me. What I might have to sacrifice is not my good but my egotistical self-centeredness, which is not good for me anyway. I begin to experience my good as identical with the common good when I have started to sideline my ego and to experience my oneness with all others. Only then will I be free to live and work for the common good or, in other words, to do God's will.

This does not mean that the individual is not uniquely valuable. We have seen how Jesus valued each individual he met. What we are saying is that the common good is ultimately in the best interests of each unique and irreplaceable individual.

Of course, the concept of the common good has often been exploited and misused to crush the individual or to ignore his or her rights. Oppressive governments do this all the time. But it is a misuse of the idea of the common good. The selfish interests of the ruling elite are presented as good for everyone, and those who disagree have to be sacrificed for it. But this is precisely what the common good does not mean. When Caiaphas the high priest says of Jesus, "It is better...to have one man die for the people than to have the whole nation destroyed" (Jn 11:50), he is hopelessly wrong about what is best for the nation.[5]

Jesus spoke about the common good as the will of God. God wants what is best for all of us and for the universe as a whole. There was no conflict between what Jesus wanted and what God wanted. That is true freedom. In the final analysis, radical freedom is the freedom to work for the common good, which might also be described as participating willingly and creatively in *God's Work*.

## God's Work

For Jesus, God's Work was in the first place the original and ongoing work of creation. For us today it is the original burst of energy, the exploding stars, the expanding universe, and the creative diversity that we witness all around us. The entire magnificent, evolutionary universe is God's Work.

The developmental history of the human species is also God's Work. The planting of the seeds of the family-kingdom in Jesus' time and their slow, uneven growth since then are all part of God's Work. Among us today, God's Work becomes visible in the signs of our times. In the hunger for spirituality and for healing we can see the finger of God. God is at work in the ongoing history of structural change and in the globalization of the struggle for justice. The new movement for peace and the quiet development of compassion for all are clearly part of God's Work in our times. Jesus would have been delighted to hear the newly articulate voices of the marginalized, the victims, the poor, and the oppressed. God is at work there too.

The healing of the human is God's Work. Nature heals, we say. The doctor simply dresses the wounds and makes supports for the broken bones. Nature provides the actual healing. Much of what has been said in this book has been a "doctoring" of our wounds and our brokenness. In the end, God does the healing.

The great work that Thomas Berry describes as "the transition from a period of human devastation of the Earth to a period when humans would be present to the planet in a mutually beneficial manner,"[6] is, he says, "the task not simply of the human community, but of the entire planet Earth. Even beyond Earth, it is the Great Work of the universe itself."[7] In other words, this too is God's Work. It is God who will save the planet and the human species—if they are to be saved. Much depends upon whether we humans participate in God's Great Work or not.

If we fail to cooperate, the ego might triumph and our species, among others, might become extinct—the sixth extinction. But the rest of the universe will continue, and God's limitless creativity will take the universe to yet greater heights without us—as a species. We do not know what the future holds, but we do know that God's Work will continue.

## Free to Do God's Work

Jesus challenges us to participate in God's Work—as he did. This is not how we commonly see things. What needs to be done has commonly been seen as *our* work. God enters into the picture as someone who can *help us do our work.* We must pray, it is said, for God's grace. In fact what needs to be done is God's Work and it is we who can be said to help by participating in God's Great Work. God's grace or free gift is best seen as the privilege of participating.

But first we need to become free and humble enough to do so. We need to recognize that we ourselves are products of

God's Work, creatures among other creatures. We are God's handiwork, a small but unique part of God's great ongoing work of art. But we are also invited to participate in the process by becoming co-artists and co-creators of the future.

We do this by allowing God to work in and through us. When we are radically free or on the way to radical freedom, divine energy can flow through us *unhindered*. This divine energy, which is also called the Holy Spirit, is infinitely powerful, creative, and healing. We see it at work in the prophets, the mystics, and the saints, but above all in Jesus. The Holy Spirit is Jesus' spirit.

In Jesus we see an unlimited self-confidence that was not a display of ego but a manifestation of radical freedom. His complete trust in God enabled the divine, creative energy of the universe to perform extraordinary miracles of healing in the people around him. Francis of Assisi was physically weak and sickly. At times he could hardly stand on his two feet, but that did not hinder the energy, the desire, and the determination that drove him on.

We can do the same. We can give up doing our own thing and begin to participate in the only work that is effective and real: God's Work. That may include many of the things we are already doing, but in a new way, with new motivation. Most highly motivated people are motivated by their egos. When we sideline the ego we can go through a period of feeling unmotivated or de-motivated, until one day we begin to experience a form of motivation that is unstoppable because it is the Work of God. One's personal transformation, in the final analysis, is also God's Work.

God's Work, like God's Wisdom, is revolutionary. It turns the world upside down. We participate by adding our voices to the many prophetic voices that are speaking out boldly in our day and age. There are countless numbers of people around the world who are doing God's Work. The challenge we face is to join them, if we have not already done so.

Jesus' Way is a path that will lead us to freedom, the radical freedom that enables us to participate in God's Great Work of Art—freely, spontaneously, creatively, and together.

Most of us are not there yet. As a species we have only just begun to evolve. We still have a long way to go. But this should not tempt us to give up any sense of urgency. The hungry need to be fed immediately. Poverty and disease need to be eliminated without delay. The greenhouse gas emissions should be stopped now. The struggle against selfishness is a matter of extreme urgency. It is all God's Work, and our participation in it cannot be postponed. A new sense of patient urgency will develop as we grow day by day in inner freedom.

God's Work sometimes appears to be very slow. Perhaps that is because we do not always appreciate the immensity of what we are involved in. Yet, precisely because it is God's Work, the future is secure. There is hope for the universe and for each of us as individuals. When I die, my ego, my false self, will be destroyed once and for all, but my true self will continue forever in God, the Self of the universe.

# Notes

## Introduction

1. See especially Richard A. Horsley and Neil Asher Silberman, *The Message and the Kingdom: How Jesus and Paul Ignited a Revolution and Transformed the Ancient World* (Minneapolis: Augsburg Fortress, 2002), 1–7 and elsewhere; and also Richard A. Horsley, *Jesus and the Spiral of Violence: Popular Jewish Resistance in Roman Palestine* (San Francisco: Harper and Row, 1987). Elizabeth A. Johnson has made brilliant use of the latest archaeological discoveries in order to reconstruct life in Mary's village of Nazareth in *Truly Our Sister: A Theology of Mary in the Communion of Saints* (New York: Continuum, 2003), 137–206.

2. See for example John Dominic Crossan, *The Historical Jesus: The Life of a Mediterranean Jewish Peasant* (Edinburgh: T. & T. Clark, 1991).

## 1. Hunger for Spirituality

1. It is the biggest selling novel *for adults*. The Harry Potter books are the biggest selling novels ever *for children*, although they are also read by millions of adults.

2. For a brief summary of the many criticisms, see Gerard O'Collins, "Da Vinci Fraud," *The Pastoral Review* 1, no. 5 (2005): 71–74.

3. In chapter 7 we will explore briefly the role of Mary Magdalene in the life of Jesus.

4. We will explore the mechanistic worldview in chapter 4.

5. Joanna Macy, *World as Lover, World as Self* (Berkeley: Parallax Press, 1991), 15.

6. David Tacey, *The Spirituality Revolution: The Emergence of Contemporary Spirituality* (New York: Brunner-Routledge, 2004), 11.

7. See for example Don Cupitt, *Mysticism after Modernity* (Malden, MA and Oxford: Blackwell, 1998), 3–6 and elsewhere.

8. Ibid., 15–23.

9. Diarmuid O'Murchu, *Reclaiming Spirituality: A New Spiritual Framework for Today's World* (Dublin: Gill and Macmillan, 1997), vii, 53, 75; *idem, Religion in Exile: A Spiritual Vision for the Homeward Bound* (Dublin: Gill and Macmillan, 2000), 6–7,18, 65–70. See Cletus Wessels' criticism of this in *The Holy Web: Church and the New Universe Story* (Maryknoll, NY: Orbis, 2000), 116–17.

10. Tacey, *The Spirituality Revolution*, 30, 36–37, 75.

11. Ibid., 24–25.

12. Ibid., 68.

13. William Bloom, *Soulution: The Holistic Manifesto* (Carlsbad, CA: Hay House, 2004).

14. Tacey, *The Spirituality Revolution*, 11, 78.

15. Ibid., 114–15.

## 2. The Crisis of Individualism

1. Stephen B. Scharper, *Redeeming the Time: A Political Theology of the Environment* (New York: Continuum,1998), 96, summarizing the thought of Catherine Keller.

2. Robert Bellah et al., *Habits of the Heart: Individualism and Commitment in American Life* (Berkeley, CA: University of California Press, 1985), 142–63.

3. Neville Symington, *A Pattern of Madness* (London: Karnac, 2002).

4. Ken Wilber, *Boomeritis: A Novel That Will Set You Free* (Boston: Shambhala, 2005).

5. David Tacey, *The Spirituality Revolution: The Emergence of Contemporary Spirituality* (New York: Brunner-Routledge, 2004), 145.

6. Ian Linden, *A New Map of the World* (London: Darton, Longman and Todd, 2003), 16–34, 148.

7. Bellah et al., *Habits of the Heart,* vii.

8. Ibid,, 284.

9. David Toolan, *At Home in the Cosmos* (Maryknoll, NY: Orbis, 2001), 79–91.

10. Michael McCarthy, "Sloughing Towards Disaster," *The Tablet*, London, 12 February 2005, 9.

11. Joanna Macy, *World as Lover, World as Self* (Berkeley, CA: Parallax Press, 1991), 183.

### 3. Globalization from Below

1. Dorothee Soelle, *Suffering* (Philadelphia: Fortress, 1975), 18–32.

2. Ibid., 70.

3. Ian Linden, *A New Map of the World* (London: Darton, Longman and Todd, 2003), 37–51.

4. I have not been able to verify these figures. By now the figures may be even higher than this.

5. For information about books and articles on the American Empire, see www.thirdworldtraveler.com.

6. This is the well-known theory of violence expounded by the French writer and thinker René Girard.

7. See René Girard, *I See Satan Fall Like Lightning* (Maryknoll, NY: Orbis, 2001), 161–69. See also Gil Bailie, *Violence Unveiled: Humanity at the Crossroads* (New York: Crossroad, 1997), 18–29.

8. For this and other examples of women on different sides of a conflict working together for peace, see Marigold Best and Pamela Hussey, *A Culture of Peace: Women, Faith and Reconciliation* (London: CIIR, 2005).

9. Girard, *I See Satan Fall Like Lightning*, 169.

10. More information about the WSF can be accessed on the Internet.

### 4. Science after Einstein

1. Bill Bryson, *A Short History of Nearly Everything* (London: Doubleday, 2003), 161.

2. Brian Swimme, *The Hidden Heart of the Cosmos: Humanity and the New Story* (Maryknoll, NY: Orbis, 1996), 93.

3. Ibid., 100.

4. David Bohm, *Wholeness and the Implicate Order* (London and New York: Routledge, 1980).

5. Quoted in Bryson, *A Short History,* 36.

6. Fritjof Capra, *The Hidden Connections: A Science for Sustainable Living* (New York: Doubleday, 2002), 30. See also his *Uncommon Wisdom: Conversations with Remarkable People* (New York: Simon and Schuster, 1988), 84–85.

7. Louis Roy, *Mystical Consciousness: Western Perspectives and Dialogue with Japanese Thinkers* (Albany, NY: State University of New York Press, 2003), 37–39.

## 5. A Revolution

1. Richard A. Horsley and Neil Asher Silberman, *The Message and the Kingdom: How Jesus and Paul Ignited a Revolution and Transformed the Ancient World* (Minneapolis: Augsburg Fortress, 2002), 60–62.

2. Richard A. Horsley, *Jesus and the Spiral of Violence: Popular Jewish Resistance in Roman Palestine* (San Francisco: Harper and Row, 1987), 324.

3. See Albert Nolan, *Jesus Before Christianity,* 25th anniversary ed. (Maryknoll, NY: Orbis, 2001), 62–66.

4. Ibid., 67–72.

5. The story of Mary Magdalene will be taken up in chapter 7.

6. This story was undoubtedly added to the gospels later by someone who thought, quite rightly, that it expressed very well Jesus' general attitude to punishment for sin. Some manuscripts don't have it at all, some place it here, others after John 7:36 or after John 21:25 or after Luke 21:38.

7. John Dominic Crossan, *The Dark Interval: Towards a Theology of Story* (Chicago: Argus, 1975), 48–62.

8. For an analysis of the Holiness Code, see Albert Nolan, *God in South Africa* (Cape Town: David Phillip, 1988), 34–38.

9. George M. Soares-Prabhu, *The Dharma of Jesus* (Maryknoll, NY: Orbis, 2003), 93.

10. Richard A. Horsley, *Jesus and the Spiral of Violence,* 190–93; Roger Haight, *Jesus Symbol of God* (Maryknoll, NY: Orbis, 1999), 65.

11. See Nolan, *Jesus Before Christianity,* 76.

12. Wes Howard-Brook, *The Church Before Christianity* (Maryknoll, NY: Orbis, 2001), 72.

13. Sara Parvis, "The Open Family: Kinship in the Bible and the Pre-Reformation Church," *The Pastoral Review* 1, no. 3 (2005): 34.

14. John Dominic Crossan has argued convincingly for Jesus' vision of the kingdom as a present reality. See *The Historical Jesus: The Life of a Mediterranean Jewish Peasant* (Edinburgh: T. & T. Clark, 1991), 276–87, 345.

15. René Girard, *I See Satan Fall Like Lightning* (Maryknoll, NY: Orbis, 2001), 123–31.

16. See my analysis of these texts in *Jesus Before Christianity,* 138.

### 6. A Prophet and a Mystic

1. Some New Testament scholars believe that this prophecy of the fall of Jerusalem was written after it happened in 70 CE. However, I am inclined to think that Jesus did make this prediction. See Albert Nolan, *Jesus Before Christianity,* 25th anniversary ed. (Maryknoll, NY: Orbis, 2001), 21–23. But whether he did or not, the concern for the women and children is typical of Jesus' spirituality.

2. My earlier assertion that Jesus was middle-class because he was the son of a carpenter (*Jesus Before Christianity,* 27) has now been shown to be incorrect. See especially Dominic Crossan's *The Historical Jesus: The Life of a Mediterranean Jewish Peasant* (Edinburgh: T. & T. Clark, 1991) and Richard A. Horsley, *Jesus and the Spiral of Violence: Popular Jewish Resistance in Roman Palestine* (San Francisco: Harper and Row, 1987).

3. See Richard Horsley's brilliant study of this in *Jesus and the Spiral of Violence.*

4. Gerhard Von Rad, *The Message of the Prophets,* trans. D. M. G. Stalker (New York: Harper and Row, 1972; London: SCM, 1968), 42, 50, 165–66.

5. It seems to me to be unlikely that the early Christian communities would have thought up the idea of Jesus being tempted if he had not said something about it himself.

6. Nolan, *Jesus Before Christianity,* 27.

7. Ibid., 93–97.

8. Jesus' union with God is generally spoken of as the hypostatic union, that is to say, the union of the divine and the human in one person, and his relationship to the Father as the relation between two persons of the Trinity. This makes Jesus the only-begotten Son of God and all others, like the mystics, the adopted sons and daughters of God.

9. For a summary of the latest scholarship on Jesus' use of the term *abba*, see Roger Haight, *Jesus Symbol of God* (Maryknoll, NY: Orbis, 1999), 100–101.

10. Edward Schillebeeckx, *Jesus: An Experiment in Christology*, trans. Hubert Hoskins (London: Collins, 1979), 260.

11. James D. G. Dunn, *Christology in the Making* (Philadelphia: Westminster Press, 1980), 26.

12. Robert Hamilton-Kelly, *God the Father: Theology and Patriarchy in the Teaching of Jesus* (Philadelphia: Fortress, 1979), 81.

13. Schillebeeckx, *Jesus*, 266, 268.

14. David Tracy, "Recent Catholic Spirituality: Unity amid Diversity," in *Christian Spirituality: Post-Reformation and Modern*, vol. 3 (London: SCM, 1990), 160–70. See also Philip F. Sheldrake, "Christian Spirituality as a Way of Living Publicly: A Dialectic of the Mystical and Prophetic," *Spiritus: Journal of Christian Spirituality* 3, no. 1 (2003), 24–27.

15. See Robert Ellsberg, *All Saints: Daily Reflections on Saints, Prophets, and Witnesses for Our Time* (New York: Crossroad, 1997).

16. See Horsley's very interesting argument for the historicity of Jesus' appointment of the twelve apostles in *Jesus and the Spiral of Violence*, 199–208.

17. Even if the words of Mark 10:42-45 are the words of the early church rather than Jesus himself, they capture very well the spirit of Jesus' teaching and spirituality.

18. Karl Rahner, *The Practice of the Faith* (New York: Crossroad, 1983), 22.


### 7. A Spirituality of Healing

1. Marcus J. Borg, *Meeting Jesus Again for the First Time: The Historical Jesus and the Heart of Contemporary Faith* (San Francisco: HarperSanFrancisco, 1994), 31.

2. J. D. Crossan, *The Historical Jesus: The Life of a Mediterranean Jewish Peasant* (Edinburgh: T. & T. Clark, 1991), xii.

3. See my attempt at analyzing Jesus' miracles in *Jesus Before Christianity,* 25th anniversary ed. (Maryknoll, NY: Orbis, 2001), 40–44.

4. Mark followed by Matthew and Luke has made this into a story that proves that Jesus has authority to forgive sins.

5. See René Girard's *The Scapegoat* (Baltimore: John Hopkins University Press, 1986) for a brilliant analysis of this mechanism.

6. Even if Jesus did not actually utter these words from the cross, they express very well his general attitude of forgiveness rather than blame.

7. Crossan, *The Historical Jesus,* 220–24.

8. I do not think that Jesus' saying that Simon did not kiss him or anoint his feet is meant as a criticism. It is simply a comparison between the reactions of someone who has been forgiven much and someone who believes he has little need of forgiveness.

9. The statements to this effect in Mark 2:7 and Matthew 9:6 and parallel texts are clearly redactional.

10. The moralizing tendency of the gospel writers has crept into some texts. They tend to make our forgiving one another a *condition* for being forgiven by God. How this crept in is well demonstrated by George M. Soares-Prabhu in *The Dharma of Jesus* (Maryknoll, NY: Orbis, 2003), 222–23.

11. About this story see note 6 in chapter 5.

12. The judgment stories in the gospels are simply trying to distinguish the kind of behavior that would be justifiable from the kind of behavior that would not be. The punishment in prison, or outer darkness with gnashing of teeth, or Hades, or hellfire is not to be taken literally. This kind of punishment was probably part of the moralizing editing of the gospel writers. Taken literally, these verses would contradict all that Jesus ever said about God's love.

13. See for example Elisabeth Schüssler Fiorenza, *In Memory of Her: A Feminist Theological Reconstruction of Christian Origins* (New York: Crossroad; London: SCM, 1983), 332–33; Sandra M. Schneiders, *Written That You May Believe: Encountering Jesus in the Fourth Gospel,* rev. and expanded ed. (New York: Crossroad, 2003), 244–45; and Sandra M. Rushing, *The Magdalene Legacy: Exploring the Wounded Icon of Sexuality* (London: Bergin & Garvey, 1994). For an overview of the upsurge

of interest in Mary Magdalene, see Ed Conroy, "Resurrecting Mary Magdalene," in *National Catholic Reporter* (July 15, 2005), 11–13.

14. See Rushing, *The Magdalene Legacy*, 51–54.

15. See Nolan, *Jesus Before Christianity*, 37–40.

## 8. In Silence and Solitude

1. Anthony Storr, *Solitude* (London: HarperCollins, 1989).

2. See for example Basil Pennington, *Centering Prayer: Renewing an Ancient Christian Prayer Form* (New York: Doubleday, 1980).

3. William Johnston, *Silent Music: The Science of Meditation* (London: Collins, 1977), 55.

4. Thomas Merton, *Contemplative Prayer* (London: Darton, Longman and Todd, 1973), 112.

5. I have been unable to trace this in the works of Eckhart and I no longer remember where I read it. For an excellent account of the importance of silence for all the mystics, see Dorothee Soelle, *The Silent Cry: Mysticism and Resistance* (Minneapolis: Augsburg Fortress, 2001), 70–76.

6. The spirituality of the present moment has been popularized in recent years by Eckhart Tolle's book *The Power of Now: A Guide to Spiritual Enlightenment*, rev. ed. (London: Hodder & Stoughton, 2005). For the importance of this idea in Christianity and Buddhism, see Brian Pierce, *We Walk the Path Together: Learning from Thich Nhat Hanh and Meister Eckhart* (Maryknoll, NY: Orbis, 2005), 21–24.

## 9. Getting to Know Oneself

1. Neville Symington, *A Pattern of Madness* (London: Karnac, 2002), 190.

2. Meister Eckhart, *Meister Eckhart: Sermons and Treatises,* 3 vols., ed. and trans. Maurice O'C. Walshe (Shaftesbury: Element Books, 1979), #46, 20. All subsequent references to Eckhart's sermons will appear as *Eckhart* followed by the sermon number (#) and page.

3. Another way of categorizing different personality types is the Myers-Briggs method. The reader who would like to explore the differ-

ently structured egos of the enneagram might try reading Sandra Maitri's *The Spiritual Dimension of the Enneagram: Nine Faces of the Soul* (New York: Penguin Putnam, 2000) or A. H. Almaas's *Facets of Unity: The Enneagram of Holy Ideas* (Berkeley, CA: Diamond Books, 1998).

4. The ego's cunning is beautifully described by Dag Hammarskjold in his diaries, as Dorothee Soelle points out in her book *The Silent Cry: Mysticism and Resistance* (Minneapolis: Augsburg Fortress, 2001), 225–26.

5. The English translations of the Bible have great difficulty with Paul's use of the word *sarx*. Good News translates it "human nature," NIV has "sinful nature," NEB "lower nature," the American Bible translates it as "physical cravings," and the NJB as "self-indulgence." The NRSV goes back to "the flesh."

6. Henri Nouwen, *The Inner Voice of Love: A Journey through Anguish to Freedom* (New York: Doubleday, 1996), 91.

## 10. With a Grateful Heart

1. For a discussion of this text and of thanksgiving in general in the gospels, see George M. Soares-Prabhu, *The Dharma of Jesus* (Maryknoll, NY: Orbis, 2003), 215–17.

2. This story was compiled by Luke from different pieces of tradition about Jesus, like his associating with sinners, his dining with Pharisees, and his anointing by a woman either on his head (Mk 14:3; Mt 26:7) or his feet (Jn 12:3). Luke chose the anointing of the feet and put the story together in a way that brings out Jesus' appreciation of grateful love.

3. David Steindl-Rast, *Gratefulness, the Heart of Prayer: An Approach to Life in Fullness* (Ramsey, NJ: Paulist Press, 1984), 15.

4. Ronald Rolheiser, *The Holy Longing: The Search for a Christian Spirituality* (New York: Doubleday, 1999), 66.

5. Ibid., 67.

6. Steindl-Rast, *Gratefulness*, 59.

7. Ken Wilber and his wife Treya take us through the experience of suffering, death, and bereavement (Treya died of cancer) in *Grace and Grit: Spirituality and Healing in the Life and Death of Treya Killam*

*Wilber* (Dublin: Gill and Macmillan, 2001). It is a book of extraordinary spiritual maturity.

## 11. Like a Little Child

1. J. D. Crossan, *The Historical Jesus: The Life of a Mediterranean Jewish Peasant* (Edinburgh: T. & T. Clark, 1991), 266–69.

2. A. H. Almaas, *Facets of Unity: The Enneagram of Holy Ideas* (Berkeley: Diamond Books, 1998), 22–25.

3. See Kenneth S. Leong, *The Zen Teachings of Jesus* (New York: Crossroad, 1995), 14.

4. See Mary Evelyn Tucker in *Worldly Wonder: Religions Enter Their Ecological Phase* (Chicago: Open Court, 2003), 50–54, 89, 98, 100.

5. Sally McFague, *The Body of God: An Ecological Theology* (Minneapolis: Augsburg Fortress, 1993), 122–24.

6. Evelyn Underhill, *Mysticism: A Study in the Nature and Development of Spiritual Consciousness* (Mineola, NY: Dover Publications, 2002; original edition 1911), 437–43.

7. See Leong on Jesus' humor, laughter, and joy in *The Zen Teachings of Jesus,* 14, 21.

8. Today, of course, millions upon millions of children may not display these qualities because they have been deprived of their childhood by poverty, war, malnutrition, and sexual abuse.

## 12. Letting Go

1. These instructions can be found in four places in the gospels and in each place they differ. In Luke (9:3) and Matthew (10:10) the disciples are told not to carry a staff. In Mark (6:8) they may do so. In Matthew (10:10) and Luke (10:4) they are to go without sandals. In Mark (6:9) they take one pair of sandals. The idea is clearly not a list of rules but a challenge to be detached about these things.

2. For Meister Eckhart on detachment, see *Sermons and Treatises,* Vol. III, 117–18.

3. I am indebted to taped talks by Angeles Aries for this description of detachment.

4. *Eckhart* #9, 79–81, 88–89. See Cyprian Smith's comment on this in *The Way of Paradox: Spiritual Life as Taught by Meister Eckhart* (London: Darton, Longman and Todd, 1987), 92–93.

## 13. One with God

1. See for example Gordon D. Kaufman, *In Face of Mystery: A Constructive Theology* (Cambridge MA: Harvard University Press, 1993), 60–61, 337; and on God as mystery in Rahner, Metz, Gutierrez, and Tracy, see Gaspar Martinez, *Confronting the Mystery of God* (New York: Continuum, 2001), 241–51.

2. *Eckhart* #69, 165, 169.

3. Eckhart, *Sermons and Treatises*, Vol. III, 35.

4. Irenaeus's statement on deification, "God became human that humans might become God," has been quoted by theologians and spiritual writers throughout the centuries. See also 2 Peter 1:4.

5. *Eckhart* #13b, 117; and in numerous other places.

6. Besides, in Christian theology God is spoken of as a Trinity of three persons.

7. Kaufman, *In Face of Mystery*, 368.

## 14. One with Ourselves

1. Erich Fromm, *The Art of Loving* (New York: Bantam, 1956), 52, n. 3.

2. Ken Wilber, like many others, says we are not our bodies, but he is talking about something else. What he is saying is that we must not identify our true selves with our emotions, our thoughts, or our bodies. The true self is the witness who looks at everything else in me. *The Essential Ken Wilber: An Introductory Reader* (Boston: Shambhala, 1998), 36–37.

3. See Oliver Davies, *Meister Eckhart: Mystical Theologian* (London: SPCK, 1991), 74–75.

4. See for example Diane Ackerman's beautiful book on the development of the senses: *A Natural History of the Senses* (New York: Random House, 1990).

5. In his book *Sources of the Self: The Making of the Modern Identity* (Cambridge: Harvard University Press, 1989), Charles Taylor traces this development in great detail.

## 15. One with Other Human Beings

1. One could go further and say that my identity is to be sought in my oneness with all living beings or with the entire universe, as we will see in chapter 16. But first we need to focus on our oneness and identity with other humans.

2. The DNA evidence would seem to suggest that we all come from the same ancestors or parents.

3. In the Bible generally and especially in the Gospel of John the word "flesh" is used differently from the way Paul uses it. Here it does not refer to the ego as in chapter 9 above.

4. Pumla Gobodo-Madikizela, *A Human Being Died That Night: A Story of Forgiveness* (Cape Town: David Philip, 2003).

5. See Albert Nolan, *Jesus Before Christianity,* 25th anniversary ed. (Maryknoll, NY: Orbis, 2001), 62–63.

6. See also Acts 2:44-45 and 5:1-10.

7. The importance of this collection is convincingly argued by Richard A. Horsley and Neil Asher Silberman in *The Message and the Kingdom: How Jesus and Paul Ignited a Revolution and Transformed the Ancient World* (Minneapolis: Augsburg Fortress, 2002), 184–97.

## 16. One with the Universe

1. See for example Psalms 8:1-9; 19:1-6; 29:1-11; 65:9-13; 104:1-35; 136:1-9; and 148:1-14.

2. John Dominic Crossan, *The Historical Jesus: The Life of a Mediterranean Jewish Peasant* (Edinburgh: T. & T. Clark, 1991), 295.

3. For other examples, see Evelyn Underhill, *Mysticism: A Study in the Nature and Development of Spiritual Consciousness* (Mineola, NY:

Dover Publications, 2002; original edition 1911), 191–93, 234, 254–58, 301–2; and Dorothee Soelle, *The Silent Cry: Mysticism and Resistance* (Minneapolis: Augsburg Fortress, 2001), 98–101.

4. For some examples, see Anthony Storr, *Solitude* (London: HarperCollins, 1989), 36–37.

5. Brian Swimme and Thomas Berry, *The Universe Story: From the Primordial Flaring Forth to the Ecozoic Era—A Celebration of the Unfolding of the Cosmos* (San Francisco: HarperCollins, 1992), 237.

6. Ibid., 223.

7. Ken Wilber, *Grace and Grit: Spirituality and Healing in the Life and Death of Treya Killam Wilber* (Dublin: Gill & Macmillan, 2001), 17–20.

8. See Swimme and Berry, *The Universe Story,* 71–78; and Thomas Berry, *The Dream of the Earth* (San Francisco: Sierra Club Books, 1988), 45–46, 106–7.

9. Kathleen Duffy sums up his thinking on this in "The Texture of the Evolutionary Cosmos: Matter and Spirit in Teilhard de Chardin," in *Teilhard in the 21st Century: The Emerging Spirit of Earth,* ed. Arthur Fabel and Donald St. John (Maryknoll, NY: Orbis, 2003), 139–44.

10. See Diarmuid O'Murchu's summary of this research in *Evolutionary Faith: Rediscovering God in Our Great Story* (Maryknoll, NY: Orbis, 2002), 17.

11. Berry, *The Dream of the Earth,* 199.

12. Beatrice Bruteau, *God's Ecstasy: The Creation of a Self-Creating World* (New York: Crossroad, 1997), 152–53.

13. Quoted in Sue Woodruff, *Meditations with Mechtild of Magdeburg* (Santa Fe, NM: Bear & Co., 1982), 42.

14. See Soelle, *The Silent Cry,* 103–8.

15. See for example Ronald Rolheiser, *The Holy Longing: The Search for a Christian Spirituality* (New York: Doubleday, 1999), 79–81; and Mary Conrow Coelho, *Awakening Universe, Emerging Personhood: The Power of Contemplation in an Evolving Universe* (Lima, OH: Wyndham Hall Press, 2002), 229–32.

16. Grace M. Jantzen, *God's World, God's Body* (London: Darton, Longman and Todd, 1984); and Sally McFague, *The Body of God: An Ecological Theology* (Minneapolis: Augsburg Fortress, 1993).

17. Quoted in Joanna Macy, *World as Lover, World as Self* (Berkeley, CA: Parallax Press, 1991), 11.

18.The best way to see the difference between a subject and an object is in our grammatical use of words. We can use a word as the subject of a sentence or as the object or predicate in a sentence. When we use a word as a subject we are not yet making a statement, we are simply referring to or drawing attention to something about which we will then go on to make a statement. We are using a word not to say something but simply to point to something. The subject by itself is formless and unknown.

19. See especially Brian Swimme's lectures on the DVD series *The Powers of the Universe* (Center for the Story of the Universe, 2003).

## 17. Radically Free

1. The term "stupefyingly free" was used originally of Dominic Guzman, the founder of the Dominicans. I have borrowed it to describe Jesus' even greater freedom.

2. Albert Nolan, *Jesus Before Christianity,* 25th anniversary ed. (Maryknoll, NY: Orbis, 2001), 144–45.

3. See George M. Soares-Prabhu, *The Dharma of Jesus* (Maryknoll, NY: Orbis, 2003), 89–91.

4. For a sample of the many references to the will of God or the will of the Father, see Mk 3:35; Lk 10:21; 22:42; Mt 6:10; 7:21; 18:14; Jn 4:34; Ac 21:14; Rm 12:2.

5. Of course, the author of the Fourth Gospel quotes this as a piece of irony, because in the end Jesus' death was for the common good of the nation and more than the nation, but not in the way Caiaphas had thought it would be (see Jn 11:51–52).

6. Thomas Berry, *The Great Work: Our Way into the Future* (New York: Bell Tower, 1999), 3.

7. Ibid., 195.

# Bibliography

Almaas, A. H. *Facets of Unity: The Enneagram of Holy Ideas.* Berkeley, CA: Diamond Books, 1998.

Bailie, Gil. *Violence Unveiled: Humanity at the Crossroads.* New York: Crossroad, 1997.

Barker, Gregory A., ed. *Jesus in the World's Faiths: Leading Thinkers from Five Religions Reflect on His Meaning.* Maryknoll, NY: Orbis, 2005.

Bellah, Robert, et al. *Habits of the Heart: Individualism and Commitment in American Life.* Berkeley, CA: University of California Press, 1985.

Berry, Thomas. *The Dream of the Earth.* San Francisco: Sierra Club Books, 1988.

———. *The Great Work: Our Way into the Future.* New York: Bell Tower, 1999.

Boff, Leonardo. *Ecology and Liberation: A New Paradigm.* Maryknoll, NY: Orbis, 1995.

Bohm, David. *Wholeness and the Implicate Order.* London and New York: Routledge, 1980.

Borg, Marcus J. *Meeting Jesus Again for the First Time: The Historical Jesus and the Heart of Contemporary Faith.* San Francisco: HarperSanFrancisco, 1994.

Bruteau, Beatrice. *God's Ecstasy: The Creation of a Self-Creating World.* New York: Crossroad, 1997.

Bryson, Bill. *A Short History of Nearly Everything.* London: Doubleday, 2003.

Capra, Fritjof. *The Tao of Physics.* Boston: Shambhala, 1975.

———. *Uncommon Wisdom: Conversations with Remarkable People.* New York: Simon and Schuster, 1988.

———. *The Web of Life.* New York: Doubleday, 1996.

Capra, Fritjof and David Steindl-Rast. *Belonging to the Universe*. San Francisco: Harper, 1991.

Coelho, Mary Conrow. *Awakening Universe, Emerging Personhood: The Power of Contemplation in an Evolving Universe*. Lima, OH: Wyndham Press, 2002.

Cowan, John. *Taking Jesus Seriously: Buddhist Meditation for Christians*. Collegeville, Minnesota: Liturgical Press, 2004.

Crossan, John Dominic. *The Dark Interval: Towards a Theology of Story*. Chicago: Argus, 1975.

————. *The Historical Jesus: The Life of a Mediterranean Jewish Peasant*. Edinburgh: T. & T. Clark, 1991.

Cupitt, Don. *Mysticism after Modernity*. Malden, MA and Oxford: Blackwell, 1998.

Davies, Oliver. *Meister Eckhart: Mystical Theologian*. London: SPCK, 1991.

De Boer, Esther A. *The Gospel of Mary: Listening to the Beloved Disciple, Beyond a Gnostic and a Biblical Mary Magdalene*. London: T. & T. Clark, 2004.

Dunn, James D. G. *Christology in the Making*. Philadelphia: Westminster Press, 1980.

Eck, Suzanne. *Jetez-vous en Dieu: Initiation a Maitre Eckhardt*. Paris: Du Cerf, 2000.

Eckhart, Meister. *Meister Eckhart: Sermons and Treatises*. 3 vols., ed. and trans. Maurice O'C. Walshe. Shaftesbury, UK: Element Books, 1979.

Ellsberg, Robert. *All Saints: Daily Reflections on Saints, Prophets, and Witnesses for Our Time*. New York: Crossroad, 1997.

————. *The Saints' Guide to Happiness*. New York: North Point Press, 2003.

Fabel, Arthur and Donald St. John, eds. *Teilhard in the 21st Century: The Emerging Spirit of Earth*. Maryknoll, NY: Orbis, 2003.

Finley, James. *Merton's Palace of Nowhere: A Search for God through the Awareness of the True Self*. Notre Dame, IN: Ave Maria Press, 1978.

Freeman, Laurence. *Jesus the Teacher Within*. New York: Continuum, 2001.

Fromm, Erich. *The Art of Loving*. New York: Bantam, 1956.

Funk, Robert W. and the Jesus Seminar. *The Gospel of Jesus according to the Jesus Seminar.* Santa Rosa, CA: Polebridge Press, 1999.

Girard, René. *I See Satan Fall Like Lightning.* Maryknoll, NY: Orbis, 2001.

————. *The Scapegoat.* Baltimore: John Hopkins University Press, 1986.

Haight, Roger. *Jesus Symbol of God.* Maryknoll, NY: Orbis, 1999.

Horsley, Richard A. *Jesus and the Spiral of Violence: Popular Jewish Resistance in Roman Palestine.* San Francisco: Harper and Row, 1987.

Horsley, Richard A. and Neil Asher Silberman. *The Message and the Kingdom: How Jesus and Paul Ignited a Revolution and Transformed the Ancient World.* Minneapolis: Augsburg Fortress, 2002.

Hughes, Gerard W. *God in All Things: The Sequel to the God of Surprises.* London: Hodder & Stoughton, 2003.

Johnson, Elizabeth A. *Truly Our Sister: A Theology of Mary in the Communion of Saints.* New York: Continuum, 2003.

Johnston, William. *Silent Music: The Science of Meditation.* London: Collins, 1977.

Kaufman, Gordon D. *In Face of Mystery: A Constructive Theology.* Cambridge, MA: Harvard University Press, 1993.

King, Robert H. *Thomas Merton and Thich Nhat Hanh: Engaged Spirituality in an Age of Globalization.* New York: Continuum, 2001.

Knitter, Paul F. *Introducing Theologies of Religions.* Maryknoll, NY: Orbis, 2002.

Kornfield, Jack. *After the Ecstasy, the Laundry: How the Heart Grows Wise on the Spiritual Path.* London: Rider, 2000.

Leakey, Richard and Roger Lewin. *The Sixth Extinction: Biodiversity and Its Survival.* London: Weidenfeld and Nicholson, 1996.

Leong, Kenneth S. *The Zen Teachings of Jesus.* New York: Crossroad, 1995.

Linden, Ian. *A New Map of the World.* London: Darton, Longman and Todd, 2003.

Macy, Joanna. *World as Lover, World as Self.* Berkeley, CA: Parallax Press, 1991.

Maitri, Sandra. *The Spiritual Dimension of the Enneagram: Nine Faces of the Soul.* New York: Penguin Putnam, 2000.

McFague, Sally. *The Body of God: An Ecological Theology.* Minneapolis: Augsburg Fortress, 1993.

―――. *Super, Natural Christians.* Minneapolis: Augsburg Fortress, 1997.

McGinn, Bernard. *The Mystical Thought of Meister Eckhart: The Man from Whom God Hid Nothing.* New York: Crossroad, 2001.

Merton, Thomas. *Contemplative Prayer.* London: Darton, Longman and Todd, 1973.

―――. *The Inner Experience: Notes on Contemplation.* London: SPCK, 2003.

―――. *Thoughts on the East.* New York: New Directions, 1995.

Nolan Albert. *God in South Africa.* Cape Town: David Phillip, 1988.

―――. *Jesus Before Christianity.* 25th anniversary ed. Maryknoll, NY: Orbis, 2001.

Nouwen, Henri J. M. *The Inner Voice of Love: A Journey through Anguish to Freedom.* New York: Doubleday, 1996.

Nuth, Joan M. *God's Lovers in an Age of Anxiety: The Medieval English Mystics.* Maryknoll, NY: Orbis, 2001.

O'Murchu, Diarmuid. *Catching Up with Jesus: A Gospel Story for Our Time.* New York: Crossroad, 2005.

―――. *Evolutionary Faith: Rediscovering God in our Great Story.* Maryknoll, NY: Orbis, 2002.

―――. *Quantum Theology: Spiritual Implications of the New Physics.*

―――. *Reclaiming Spirituality: A New Spiritual Framework for Today's World.* Dublin: Gill and Macmillan, 1997.

―――. *Religion in Exile: A Spiritual Vision for the Homeward Bound.* Dublin: Gill and Macmillan, 2000.

Rev. and updated ed. New York: Crossroad, 2004.

Pagels, Elaine. *Beyond Belief: The Secret Gospel of Thomas.* New York: Random House, 2005.

Pierce, Brian J. *We Walk the Path Together: Learning from Thich Nhat Hanh and Meister Eckhart.* Maryknoll, NY: Orbis, 2005.

Rolheiser, Ronald. *The Holy Longing: The Search for a Christian Spirituality.* New York: Doubleday, 1999.

Roy, Louis. *Mystical Consciousness: Western Perspectives and Dialogue with Japanese Thinkers.* Albany, NY: State University Press, 2003.

Ruether, Rosemary Radford. *Gaia and God: An Ecofeminist Theology of Earth Healing*. San Francisco: Harper, 1992.

Rushing, Sandra M. *The Magdalene Legacy: Exploring the Wounded Icon of Sexuality*. London: Bergin & Garvey, 1994.

Scharper, Stephen Bede. *Redeeming the Time: A Political Theology of the Environment*. New York: Continuum, 1998.

Schillebeeckx, Edward. *Jesus: An Experiment in Christology*. Trans. Hubert Hoskins. London: Collins, 1979.

Schüssler Fiorenza, Elizabeth. *In Memory of Her: A Feminist Theological Reconstruction of Christian Origins*. New York: Crossroad, 1983.

Smith, Cyprian. *The Way of Paradox: Spiritual Life as Taught by Meister Eckhart*. London: Darton, Longman and Todd, 1987.

Soares-Prabhu, George M. *The Dharma of Jesus*. Maryknoll, NY: Orbis, 2003.

Soelle, Dorothee. *The Silent Cry: Mysticism and Resistance*. Minneapolis: Augsburg Fortress, 2001.

————. *Suffering*. Philadelphia: Fortress, 1975.

Steindl-Rast, David. *Gratefulness, the Heart of Prayer: An Approach to Life in Fullness*. Ramsey, NJ: Paulist Press, 1984.

Storr, Anthony. *Solitude*. London: HarperCollins, 1989.

Swimme, Brian. *The Hidden Heart of the Cosmos: Humanity and the New Story*. Maryknoll, NY: Orbis, 1996.

Swimme, Brian and Thomas Berry. *The Universe Story: From the Primordial Flaring Forth to the Ecozoic Era—A Celebration of the Unfolding of the Cosmos*. San Francisco: Harper, 1992.

Symington, Neville. *A Pattern of Madness*. London: Karnac, 2002.

Tacey, David. *The Spirituality Revolution: The Emergence of Contemporary Spirituality*. New York: Brunner-Routledge, 2004.

Taylor, Charles. *Sources of the Self: The Making of Modern Identity*. Cambridge: Harvard University Press, 1989.

Thorne, Brian. *Infinitely Beloved: The Challenge of Divine Intimacy*. London: Darton, Longman and Todd, 2003.

Tolle, Eckhart. *The Power of Now: A Guide to Spiritual Enlightenment*. Rev. ed. London: Hodder & Stoughton, 2005.

Toolan, David. *At Home in the Cosmos*. Maryknoll, NY: Orbis, 2001.

Tracy, David. *On Naming the Present: God, Hermeneutics, and Church*. Maryknoll, NY: Orbis, 1994.

————. "Recent Catholic Spirituality: Unity amid Diversity." In *Christian Spirituality: Vol. III, Post-Reformation and Modern.* London: SCM, 1990.

Tucker, Mary Evelyn. *Worldly Wonder: Religions Enter Their Ecological Phase.* Chicago: Open Court, 2003.

Turner, Denys. *The Darkness of God: Negativity in Christian Mysticism.* Cambridge, UK: Cambridge University Press, 1995.

Underhill, Evelyn. *Mysticism: A Study in the Nature and Development of Spiritual Consciousness.* Mineola, NY: Dover Publications, 2002. (Original edition 1911.)

Wessels, Cletus. *The Holy Web: Church and the New Universe Story.* Maryknoll, NY: Orbis, 2000.

————. *Jesus in the New Universe Story.* Maryknoll, NY: Orbis, 2003.

Wilber, Ken. *The Collected Works of Ken Wilber, Vol. 7, A Brief History of Everything and The Eye of Spirit.* Boston: Shambhala, 2000.

————. *The Essential Ken Wilber: An Introductory Reader.* Boston: Shambhala, 1998.

————. *Grace and Grit: Spirituality and Healing in the Life and Death of Treya Killam Wilber.* Dublin: Gill & Macmillan, 2001.

# Index